The Essential

SPONTANEOUS

of FULFILLMENT

DESIRE

FUNDAMENTAL PRINCIPLES FROM THE
ORIGINAL BESTSELLING BOOK

The Essential SPONTANEOUS *of* FULFILLMENT DESIRE

THE ESSENCE OF HARNESSING THE
INFINITE POWER OF COINCIDENCE

DEEPAK CHOPRA

Harmony Books　*New York*

All rights reserved.
Published in the United States by Harmony Books, an imprint of the Crown
Publishing Group, a division of Random House, Inc., New York.
www.crownpublishing.com

This is an abridged edition of *Spontaneous Fulfillment of Desire: Harnessing the
Infinite Power of Coincidence,* published in hardcover in the United States by
Harmony Books, an imprint of the Crown Publishing Group, a division of
Random House Inc., New York, in 2003.

Harmony Books is registered trademark and the Harmony Books colophon is
a trademark of Random House, Inc.

Library of Congress Cataloging-in-Publication Data is available upon request

ISBN 978-0-307-40772-6

Printed in the United States of America

Design by Lauren Dong

10 9 8 7 6 5 4 3 2 1

First Abridged Edition

To Rita, Mallika, Gotham, Candice,
Sumant, Tara, and Leela:

You orchestrate the synchronistic
dance of my universe

Author's Note

There are few things in life that I find more gratifying than learning and teaching. We are all born with an insatiable curiosity about the world around us, and I was fortunate to grow up in a home that encouraged that appetite. Now, as an adult, I enjoy the best of both worlds: I can explore science, ancient wisdom, health, and spirit on the one hand, and on the other I can share what I've learned—helping others to satisfy their own curiosities—through my books and lectures.

When I speak to audiences, I find myself presenting my ideas in a manner that is concise or expansive depending on the length of time I have at my disposal. A five-minute segment on a morning television show requires a very different presentation from an hour on my weekly Sirius radio program, which in turn is very brief compared to one of the week-long courses I teach around the globe. It occurs to me that the same holds true for what we read. After all, we don't always have the luxury of taking the time to explore the book-long articulation of a new idea, but we might have the time, say, to take in the *essence* of that idea.

It was from this thought that the Essential series was born. This series begins with three books that have attracted substantial followings in their expanded versions: *Ageless Body, Timeless Mind: The Quantum Alternative to Growing Old; How to Know God: The Soul's Journey into the Mystery of Mysteries; The Spontaneous Fulfillment of Desire: Harnessing the Infinite Power of Coincidence*. In these new essential volumes, I have distilled the most important elements from the full-length originals. It is my hope that this series will be of value to first-time readers of my work, as well as to those who may have already read these books, but wish to be inspired by these ideas all over again.

The Essential Spontaneous Fulfillment of Desire: The Essence of Harnessing the Infinite Power of Coincidence is a book for anyone who has wondered about the significance of a moment when you were thinking about an old friend with whom you've lost contact and the phone rings; it's your friend! Or a moment when you've been deeply hoping for an event and suddenly every obstacle to your vision seems to melt away. Coincidence? Perhaps. Still, such experiences are nothing to dismiss. For the word "coincidence" means "happening at the same time," and such moments are actually glimpses of a place where everything happens at the same time, a place where past and present and future are one. This book not only shows you how you can benefit from such clues, but how you can see more and more of them as you become aware of their presence and their meaning. In this way you are opening a doorway into a realm of divine intelligence, where you can consciously create your own "good luck" in all areas of your life. It's not just coincidence. It's a gateway to fulfilling your every desire.

INTRODUCTION

MIRACLES HAPPEN EVERY DAY. NOT JUST IN RE-mote country villages or at holy sites halfway across the globe, but here, in our own lives. They bubble up from their hidden source, surround us with opportunities, and disappear.

Although we think of them as extraordinary, miracles also streak across our consciousness every day. We can choose to notice or ignore them, unaware that our destinies may hang in the balance. Tune in to the presence of miracles, and in an instant, life can be transformed into a dazzling experience, more wondrous and exciting than we could even imagine. Ignore it, and an opportunity is gone forever. The question is, Would you recognize a miracle if you saw one? If you recognized it, what would you do? And if you could somehow orchestrate your own miracles, which miracles would you choose?

Beyond your physical self, beyond your thoughts and emotions, there lies a realm within you that is pure potential; from this place anything and everything is possible. Even miracles. Especially miracles. This part of you is interwoven with everything else that exists, and with everything yet to come.

We have all experienced events that might be considered amazing or uncanny. Perhaps you were cleaning out a closet and found a gift from someone you hadn't spoken with in years; then an hour later, out of the blue, that person rings you on the phone. Or perhaps your car breaks down on the side of a deserted road, and just when you had resigned yourself to being stranded for hours, the very first vehicle that comes along is a tow truck.

Can such moments be ascribed to mere coincidence? Of course they can, but on closer examination they can also prove to be glimpses of the miraculous. Each time we have an experience like these, we can choose to dismiss it as a random occurrence in a chaotic world, or we can recognize it for the potentially life-altering event it may prove to be. I do not believe in meaningless coincidences. I believe every coincidence is a message, a clue about a particular facet of our lives that requires our attention.

When you live your life with an appreciation of coincidences and their meanings, you connect with the underlying field of infinite possibilities. This is when the magic begins. This is a state I call *synchrodestiny*, in which it becomes possible to achieve the spontaneous fulfillment of our every desire. Synchrodestiny requires gaining access to a place deep within yourself, while at the same time awakening to the intricate dance of coincidences out in the physical world. It requires understanding the profound nature of things, recognizing the wellspring of intelligence that endlessly creates our universe, and yet having the intention to pursue specific opportunities for change as they appear.

MY FATHER SERVED in the Indian army as personal physician of Lord Mountbatten, the last Governor-General of the British Empire in India. While performing his duties my father spent a great deal of time with Lady Mountbatten, and they became friends. Through this friendship my father was encouraged to apply for a scholarship to become a Fellow of the Royal College of Physicians, which took him away to England when I was about six years old. Soon after, my mother also left India to join my father for a while, and my younger brother and I were left in the care of our grandparents.

One day, my father sent a telegram from England saying that he had finally passed all his examinations. This was a momentous day for everyone. My grandfather, so proud of his accomplished son, took us out to celebrate. The whole day was a glorious whirlwind of happiness. But later that night, my brother and I were awakened by the sound of wailing. Although we did not learn this immediately, my grandfather had died, and the sound that had woken us was the anguished cry of women in mourning.

This affected my brother and me profoundly. I lay awake nights wondering where my grandfather was, and whether his soul had survived in some way after his death. My brother had a different reaction—his skin started peeling, as though from a bad sunburn. There was no physical reason for this, so we consulted several doctors. One wise physician recognized that the recent traumatic events in our lives may have left my brother feeling vulnerable and exposed, and that peeling skin was an outward sign of his vulnerability. He predicted that the peeling would stop when my parents returned to India. And, indeed, when they returned, it disappeared.

Looking back I can see that these early events were the seeds of my life's work—my search to understand the nature of the soul, and my studies of the mind-body connection in health.

Seeing the web of coincidence in our lives, however, is just the first stage in understanding and living synchrodestiny. The next stage is to develop an awareness of coincidences while they are happening. It is easy to see them in hindsight, but if you catch coincidences at the moment they occur, you are better positioned to take advantage of the opportunities they may be presenting. Also, awareness translates into energy. The more attention you give to coincidences, the more likely they are to appear, which means you begin to gain greater and greater access to the messages being sent to you about the path and direction of your life.

The final stage of living synchrodestiny occurs when you become fully aware of the interrelatedness of all things, how each affects the next, how they all are "in sync" with one another. "In sync" is a colloquial way of saying "in synchrony," which means operating in unison, as one. Picture a school of fish swimming in one direction, and then in a flash, all the fish change direction. There is no leader giving directions. The fish don't think, "The fish in front of me turned left, so I should turn left." It all happens simultaneously. This synchrony is choreographed by a great, pervasive intelligence that lies at the heart of nature, and is manifest in each of us through what we call the soul.

When we learn to live from the level of the soul, many things happen. We become aware of the exquisite patterns and synchronous rhythms that govern all life. We understand the lifetimes of memory and experience that have molded us into the people we are today. Fearfulness and anxiety fall away as we stand in wonder observing the world as it unfolds. We notice the web of coincidence that surrounds us, and we realize that there is meaning in even the smallest events. We discover that by applying attention and intention to these coincidences, we can create specific outcomes in our lives. We connect with everyone and everything in the universe, and recognize the spirit that unites us all. We unveil the wondrousness that is hidden deep inside us and revel in our newfound glory. We consciously shape our destinies into the limitlessly creative expressions they were meant to be, and by doing so we live out our most profound dreams, moving closer to enlightenment.

This is the miracle of synchrodestiny.

THIS BOOK WILL not change your life overnight, but if you are willing to devote a little time every day, you will find that miracles are not only possible, they are abundant. Miracles can happen every day, every hour, every minute of your life. At this moment, the seeds of a perfect destiny lie dormant within you. Release their potential and live a life more wondrous than any dream. Let me show you how.

the
PROMISE
of UNLIMITED
POTENTIAL

I

Matter, Mind, and Spirit

From the moment we become aware of the world around us, we begin to wonder about our place within it. The questions we ask are timeless: Why am I here? How do I fit into the scheme of things? What is my destiny? As children, we tend to think of the future as a clean sheet of paper upon which we can write our own stories. The possibilities seem endless, and we are energized by the promise of discovery and the sheer pleasure of living immersed in so much potential. But as we grow up, become adults, and are "educated" about our limitations, our view of the future becomes constricted. What once lifted our imaginations now weighs us down with dread and anxiety. What once felt boundless becomes narrow and dark.

There is a way to regain the soaring joy of unlimited potential. All that is required is an understanding of the true nature of reality, a willingness to recognize the interrelatedness and inseparability of all things. Then, aided by specific techniques, you will find the world opening up to you, and the good luck and opportunities that popped up every once in a while will occur more and more frequently.

The first step to living this way is to understand the nature of the three levels of existence.

Level 1

THE PHYSICAL DOMAIN

The first level of existence is physical or material, the visible universe. This is the world we know best, what we call the real world. It contains matter and objects with firm boundaries, everything that is three-dimensional, and it includes everything we experience with our five senses—all that we can see, hear, feel, taste, or smell. In the physical domain time seems to flow in a line so straight that we call it the arrow of time, from the past to the present to the future. This means that everything in the physical domain has a beginning, a middle, and an end, and is therefore impermanent.

The physical world as we experience it is governed by immutable laws of cause and effect, so that everything is predictable. Scientists can calculate precisely when a solar eclipse will occur and how long it will last. All of our "commonsense" understanding of the world comes from what we know of this physical domain.

Level 2

THE QUANTUM DOMAIN

At the second level of existence everything consists of information and energy. This is called the quantum domain. Everything at this level is insubstantial, meaning that it cannot be touched or perceived by any of the five senses. Your mind, your thoughts, your ego, the part of you that you typically think of as your "self" are all part of the quantum domain. These things have no solidity, and yet you know your self and your thoughts to be real. Although it is easiest to think of the quantum domain in terms of mind, it encompasses much more. In fact, everything in the visible universe is a manifestation of the energy and information of the quantum domain. The material world is a subset of the quantum world.

One of the first science lessons taught in school is that every solid object is made up of molecules, and molecules are made up of even smaller units called atoms. We come to understand that this seemingly solid chair we are sitting on is made up of atoms so small that they cannot be seen without the aid of a powerful microscope. Later in the lesson we learn that tiny atoms are made up of subatomic particles, which have no solidity at all. They are, quite literally, packets or waves of information and energy. This means that, at this second level of existence, the chair you are sitting in is nothing but energy and information.

This concept can be difficult to grasp at first. How can invisible waves of energy and information be experienced as a solid object? The answer is that events in the quantum domain occur at the speed of light, and at that speed our senses simply cannot process everything that contributes to our perceptual experience. We perceive objects as being different from one to the next because energy waves contain different kinds of information, which are determined by the frequency or vibration of those energy waves.

So the physical world, the world of objects and

matter, is made up of nothing but information contained in energy vibrating at different frequencies. The reason we don't see the world as a huge web of energy is that it is vibrating far too fast. Our senses, because they function so slowly, are able to register only chunks of this energy and activity, and these clusters of information become "the chair," "my body," "water," and every other physical object in the visible universe.

At the quantum level, the various chunks of energy fields vibrating at different frequencies that we perceive as solid objects are all part of a collective energy field. If we were capable of perceiving everything that was happening at the quantum level, we would see that we are all part of a great "energy soup," and everything—each one of us and all the objects in the physical domain—is just a cluster of energy floating in this energy soup. At any given moment your energy field will come into contact with and affect everyone else's energy field, and each of us responds in some way to that experience. We are all expressions of this communal energy and information. Sometimes we can actually feel this connectedness. This sensation is usually very subtle, but on occasion it becomes more tangible. Most of us have had the experience of walking into a room and sensing "tension so thick you could cut it with a knife," or of being in a church or holy shrine and being engulfed by a sense of peace. That is the collective energy of the environment mingling with your own energy, which you register on some level.

AT A DEEPER level, there is really no boundary between our selves and everything else in the world. When you touch an object, it feels solid, as though there was a distinct boundary between it and you. Physicists would say that we experience that boundary as solid because everything is made up of atoms, and the solidity is the sense of atoms bumping against atoms. But consider what an atom is. An atom has a little nucleus with a large cloud of electrons around it. There is no rigid outer shell, just an electron cloud. To visualize this, imagine a peanut in the middle of a football stadium. The peanut represents the nucleus, and the stadium represents the size of the electron cloud around the nucleus. When we touch an object, we perceive solidity when the clouds of electrons meet. That is our interpretation of solidity, given the sensitivity (or relative insensitivity) of our senses. Our eyes are programmed to see objects as three-dimensional and solid. Our nerve endings are programmed to feel objects as three-dimensional and solid. In the reality of the quantum domain, however, there is no solidity.

So it is only in our consciousness that our limited senses create a solid world out of pure energy and information. But what if we could see into the quantum domain—if we had "quantum eyes"? In the quantum domain, we would see that everything we think of as solid in the physical world is actually flickering in and out of an infinite void at the speed of light. The continuity and solidity of the world exists only in the imagination, fed by senses that cannot discern the waves of energy and information that make up the quantum level of existence. In reality, we are all flickering in and out of existence all the time. If we could fine-tune our senses, we could actually see the gaps in our existence. We are here, and then not here, and then here again. The sense of continuity is held only by our memories.

So the mind is a field of energy and information. Every idea is also energy and information. You have imagined your physical body and the whole physical world into existence by perceiving energy soup as distinct physical entities. But where does the mind responsible for this imagination come from?

Level 3

THE NONLOCAL DOMAIN

The third level of existence consists of intelligence, or consciousness. This can be called the virtual domain, the spiritual domain, the field of potential, the universal being, or nonlocal intelligence. This is where information and energy emerge from a sea of possibilities. The most fundamental, basic level of nature is not material; it is not even energy and information soup; it is pure potential. This level of nonlocal reality operates beyond the reach of space and time, which simply do not exist at this level. We call it nonlocal because it cannot be confined by a location—it is not "in" you or "out there." It simply is.

The intelligence of the spiritual domain is what organizes "energy soup" into knowable entities. It is what binds quantum particles into atoms, atoms into molecules, molecules into structures. It is the organizing force behind all things. This can be a slippery concept to grasp. One relatively simple way of thinking about this virtual domain is to recognize the dual nature of your own thoughts. As you read these words, your eyes are seeing the black print on the page, and your mind is translating the print into symbols—

letters and words—and then trying to deduce their meaning. But take a step back and ask, Who is it that is doing the reading? What is the consciousness that underlies your thoughts? Become aware of the duality of these interior processes. Your mind is busy decoding, analyzing, and translating. So who is doing the reading? With this one little twist of attention you may become aware that there is a presence within you, a force that is always doing the experiencing. This is the soul, or nonlocal intelligence, and its experience takes place at the virtual level.

Nonlocal intelligence is everywhere at once, and can cause multiple effects simultaneously in various locations. It is from this virtual domain that everything in the world is organized and synchronized. This, then, is the source of the coincidences that are so important to synchrodestiny. When you learn to live from this level, you can spontaneously fulfill your every desire. You can create miracles.

EVIDENCE FOR THE VIRTUAL DOMAIN

The virtual domain is not a figment of the imagination, the result of some human longing for a universal force greater than ourselves. Although philosophers have been discussing and debating the existence of "spirit" for thousands of years, it wasn't until the twentieth century that science could offer proof of the existence of nonlocal intelligence.

As most of us learned in science class, the universe is made up of both solid particles and waves. We were taught that particles were the building blocks of all the solid objects in the world. For example, we learned that the very smallest units of matter, such as the electrons in an atom, were particles. Similarly, we were taught that waves—such as sound and light waves—were nonsolid. There was never confusion between the two; particles were particles, and waves were waves.

Physicists then discovered that a subatomic particle is part of what is known as a wave packet. Although waves of energy are typically continuous, with equally spaced peaks and troughs, a wave packet is a concentration of energy. (Imagine a little ball of static, with quick, sharp peaks and troughs representing the amplitude of the wave.)

There are two questions we might ask about the particle in this wave packet: (1) where is it, and (2) what is its momentum? Physicists discovered that you can ask one of these questions, but not both. For example, once you ask "Where is it?" and you fix a wave-particle in a location, it becomes a particle. If

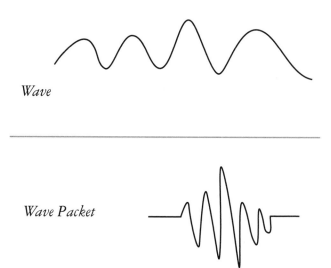

Wave

Wave Packet

you ask "What is its momentum?" you have decided that movement is the critical factor; therefore you must be talking about a wave.

So is this thing we are talking about, the "wave-particle," a particle or a wave? It depends on which of the two questions we decide to ask. At any given moment, that wave-particle can be *either* a particle *or* a wave because we can't know both the location and the momentum of the wave-particle. In fact, as it turns out, until we measure either its location or its momentum, it is *both particle and wave simultaneously.* This concept is known as the Heisenberg Uncertainty Principle, and it is one of the fundamental building blocks of modern physics.

Because observation is the key to defining the wave-particle as a single entity, Niels Bohr and other physicists believed that consciousness alone was responsible for the collapse of the wave-particle. It might be said, then, that without consciousness, everything would exist only as undefined, potential packets of energy, or pure potential.

This is one of the key points of this book. Let me repeat it because it is so important: *Without consciousness acting as an observer and interpreter, everything would exist only as pure potential.* That pure potential is the virtual domain, the third level of existence. It is non-local and can't be depleted; it is unending and all-encompassing. Tapping into that potential is what allows us to make miracles.

INTERESTING EXPERIMENTS HAVE been performed by researcher Cleve Baxter, an associate and friend of ours at the Chopra Center. In 1972 he developed a methodology for studying human cells that had been isolated from a person's body.

One day Cleve Baxter was isolating white cells in

order to study them, and a very interesting thing happened. As part of the procedure he centrifuged his saliva to get a concentrated number of white cells, then placed them in a small test tube and inserted gold wire electrodes connected to EEG-type instrumentation. He had the sudden idea to inflict a small cut on the back of his hand to see if this might affect his white cells. He went to search for a sterile lancet on a nearby shelf. When he came back he glanced at the chart that was recording the electromagnetic activity of the white blood cells: It had already registered intense activity among the white blood cells during his search for the lancet. In other words, his white cells were reacting to his *intention* to cut his hand even before he actually inflicted the cut.

But you need not go into a laboratory to see this nonlocal intelligence at work. Proof is all around us, in animals, in nature, and even in our own bodies.

SYNCHRONICITY IN NATURE

WE SEE EXAMPLES OF SYNCHRONICITY IN NATURE so often that they begin to seem ordinary. But look again with eyes that are tuned in to the near-impossibility of what's taking place, and the concept of synchronicity will begin to make sense. For example, look up at the sky on any summer's day and wait for a flock of birds. Like the school of fish I mentioned earlier, they all seem to be moving in formation; when they change direction, they all execute the same motions synchronistically. A single flock of birds can include hundreds of individuals, yet each bird moves in harmony with every other bird without an obvious leader. They change direction in an instant, all birds altering their course at the exact same moment, and they do it perfectly. How is that happening? There's not enough time for any exchange of information, so any correlation of activity among the birds must be happening nonlocally.

Physicists have been working for years to discover the properties that guide the movements of birds, and so far they have been unsuccessful. The complexity and absolute precision of the birds' behavior stumps physical science every time. The instantaneous communication we commonly see in flocks of birds and schools of fish comes from the spiritual level, the organizing nonlocal intelligence in the virtual domain. The result is synchronicity, beings that are totally in tune with their environment and with each other, dancing to the rhythm of the cosmos.

Scientist Rupert Sheldrake has conducted some fascinating studies of what seem to be cases of nonlocal communication between dogs and their human companions. People and dogs can form very close bonds, and Sheldrake has documented cases in which dogs seem to know when their owners are coming home. From ten minutes to two hours before the owner arrives, the dog will sit at the front door and wait, as if anticipating the owner's return. Skeptics have said that this was simply a case of habit, that the owner comes home at a specific time each day, or that the dog can hear the car or smell the owner from miles away. But these dogs are able to predict their owners' arrival even when he or she comes home at unexpected times, or by a different car, or on foot, or even if the wind is blowing in the opposite direction, so that there is no possible way the owner's scent could reach the house.

This doesn't happen with all dogs or all owners, but when it does, it is a very powerful phenomenon. Even more startling, Sheldrake has demonstrated that dogs can pick up on intention. Let's say the owner is in Paris on a two-week vacation, and the dog is at home in London. If the owner suddenly changes plans and decides to go home a week early, the dog shows the same signs of anticipation a week early. As soon as the owner thinks, "It's time to go home," the dog gets up from wherever he has been sleeping and sits at the front door wagging his tail, waiting for the owner's arrival.

Examples of synchronicity can be found most often in the animal world because animals are more in touch with the essential nature of things. We humans lose our sense of connectedness in a welter of concerns about rent payments, which car to buy, or any of a million other distractions. As soon as we develop an ego, a sense of "I" that is different from everyone else, those connections are obscured.

But some people do experience strong synchronicity, and they don't need to be meditators. We've all heard stories of identical twins who can readily tune in to what the other twin is feeling or thinking. This same kind of connection can be seen in other strongly bonded individuals. I was talking with a patient once when he suddenly had a piercing pain in his abdomen and began rolling around on the floor. When I asked what happened, he replied, "It feels like somebody stabbed me over here." Later we found out that at that precise moment his mother had been mugged in Philadelphia and stabbed in the abdomen. He had a very strong connection to his mother; it was easily the most important relationship in his life. They were so closely attuned that, at some level, their physiology was as one. We could say that they were *entrained*.

Entrainment is just another word for *correlation* or *synchronization;* it is used most often by scientists to describe the state of being "caught up" by another substance or force. For example, particles can be entrained in a stream of liquid and flow along immersed in it. The word helps us describe how things become correlated with each other. Remember, synchronicity occurs only when people, animals, or objects have some close relationship, or are entrained.

How can something as real and substantial as our

bodies depend on virtual communication? Consider that the human body consists of approximately one hundred trillion cells, about one thousand cells for every bright star in the Milky Way. There are some 250 different types of cells in the human body, from the spherical simple fat cell to the thin, branching nerve cell.

In addition to doing its specific job in the body, each cell does a few million things per second just to keep functioning: creating proteins, adjusting the permeability of its membrane, and processing nutrients, to name just a few. Each cell also has to know what every other cell is doing; otherwise your body would fall apart. The human body can function only if it is operating synchronistically, and all this can happen only through nonlocal correlation. How else could one hundred trillion cells each doing one million things per second coordinate their activities so as to support a living, breathing human being? How else could a human body generate thoughts, remove toxins, and smile at a baby, or even make a baby, all at the same time?

The answer is that the thought originates in the virtual domain.

OUR BODIES BEHAVE synchronistically all the time.

In a healthy body, this synchronicity is perfectly regulated. Healthy people are firmly locked into these rhythms. When disease occurs, one of those rhythms has gone awry. Stress is the biggest disrupter. If you're stressed, if you're feeling hostility, your body's balance gets thrown off. Stress breaks our nonlocal connection with everything else. When you are experiencing disease ("dis-ease"), then some part of your body is beginning to get constricted. It is tuning itself out from the nonlocal field of intelligence.

There are many emotions that can cause a disruption of the electromagnetic field in the heart, but the ones that have been most precisely documented are anger and hostility. Once this synchronization is disrupted, your body starts to behave in a fragmented manner. The immune system gets suppressed, which leads to other problems, such as increased susceptibility to cancer, infections, and accelerated aging. This effect is so strong that animals can pick it up. If a dog sees a person who is harboring hostility, it will bark and act ferocious. Wherever you go, you are broadcasting who you are at this very intimate level.

But our connection with nonlocal intelligence doesn't end at the boundary of our bodies. Just as our bodies are in balance, so the universe is in balance also, and it displays that balance in rhythms or cycles.

On earth, we feel the effects of the sun in the circadian rhythm, and the effects of the moon in the lunar rhythm, as it waxes and wanes. The cycles of the moon play themselves out in our body, instantly correlating with planetary movements. The gravitational effects of the sun and moon on the earth cause ocean tides, which also affect our bodies. After all, millions of years ago we, too, were inhabitants of the ocean. When we slithered onto shore we brought some of the ocean along with us. Eighty percent of our body has the same chemical composition as the ocean we once called home, and is still affected by its tidal pull.

There are rhythms within rhythms within rhythms. And these drumbeats echo all around us and within us. We are not outsiders to the process; we are part of it, throbbing to the pulse of the universe.

Think of the universe as a single, huge organism. Its vastness is a perceptual, projected reality; even though "out there" you may be seeing a big football stadium filled with thousands of people, the real phenomenon is a small electrical impulse inside your brain that you, the nonlocal being, interpret as a football game. Yoga Vasishta, an ancient Vedic text, says, "The world is like a huge city, reflected in a mirror. So too, the universe is a huge reflection of yourself in your own consciousness."

It is, in short, the soul of all things.

3

THE NATURE OF THE SOUL

IN THE VASTNESS OF THE OCEAN, THERE IS NO ego. Seen from a great distance, from the moon or a satellite, the ocean looks calm and inanimate, a large swath of blue girdling the earth. But as we get closer and closer to the ocean itself, we see that it is in constant motion, roiled by currents and tides, eddies and waves. We see these ocean patterns as distinct entities. As each wave is created, we can watch it crest, break, and race to the shore. Yet it is impossible to separate the wave from the ocean. You cannot take a bucket, scoop out a wave, and bring it home.

When we are beginning to understand the soul, the ocean provides a wonderful analogy. Imagine the ocean as nonlocal reality, the field of infinite possibilities, the virtual level of existence that synchronizes everything. Each of us is like a wave in that ocean. We are created from it, and it makes up the very core of who we are. Just as a wave takes on a specific shape, we, too, take on intricate patterns of nonlocal reality. This vast, unending ocean of possibility is the essence of everything in the physical world. The ocean represents the nonlocal, and the wave represents the local. The two are intimately connected.

Once we define the soul as deriving from the nonlocal, or virtual, realm, then our place in the universe becomes remarkably clear: We are both local and nonlocal, an individual pattern emerging from nonlocal intelligence, which is also part of everyone and everything else. We can think of the soul, then, as having two parts. The vast, nonlocal soul exists at the virtual or spirit level. It is powerful, pure, and capable of anything. The personal, local part of the soul exists at the quantum level. This is what reaches into our daily lives and holds the essence of who we are. It, too, is powerful, pure, and capable of anything. The same unbounded potential of the infinite spirit also resides in each and every one of us. Our personal soul, which we think of when we think of our "selves," is an outcropping of the eternal soul.

If we could learn to live from the level of the soul, we would see that the best, most luminous part of ourselves is connected to all the rhythms of the universe. We would truly know ourselves as the miracle-makers we are capable of being. We would lose fear, and longing, and hatred, and anxiety, and hesitation. Living from the level of the soul means diving past the ego, past the limitations of the mind that harness us to events and outcomes in the physical world.

We are all patterns of nonlocality pretending to be people. In the end, it is all spirit.

And yet, we all *feel* quite individual, don't we? Our senses reassure us that these bodies are real, and we think our own very personal, individual thoughts. We learn, fall in love, have children, and work at our own careers. How is it that we do not feel this vast ocean churning inside us? Why do our lives feel so circumscribed? It all comes back to the three levels of existence.

At the physical level, what we call the real world, the soul is the observer in the midst of the observation. Anytime you observe something, there are three components involved. The first, which occurs in the physical world, is the object of your observation. The second, which happens at the level of the mind, is the process of observing. The third component of observation is the actual observer, which we call the soul.

We each have a soul, but because we are each

observing from a different place and a different set of experiences, we do not observe the same things in exactly the same ways. The variations in what we observe are based on our minds' interpretations. If you and I both were to observe a dog, for instance, we would have different thoughts. I may see it as a ferocious animal, and I may become afraid. You may look at the same dog and see it as a friendly companion. Our minds interpret the observation differently. When I see a dog, I run. When you see a dog, you whistle and play with it.

Interpretation happens at the level of the mind, but it is our individual souls that are conditioned by experience, and through that memory of past experience the soul influences our choices and interpretations in life. These tiny kernels or seeds of memory build up in the individual soul over a lifetime, and this combination of memory and imagination based on experience is called karma. Karma accumulates in the personal part of the soul, the wave at the core of our being, and colors it. This personal soul governs the conscience and provides a template for the kind of person each of us will turn out to be. In addition, the actions we take can affect this personal soul, and change our karma, for better or worse.

The universal, nonlocal part of the soul is not

touched by our actions, but is connected to a spirit that is pure and unchanging. In fact, the definition of *enlightenment* is "the recognition that I am an infinite being seeing and seen from, observing and observed from, a particular and localized point of view." Whatever else we are, no matter how much of a mess we may have made of our lives, it is always possible to tap into the part of the soul that is universal, the infinite field of pure potential, and change the course of our destiny. That is synchrodestiny—taking advantage of this connection between the personal soul and the universal soul to shape your life.

So the seeds of memory built by experience, our karma, help determine who we are. But the individuality of our personal soul is shaped by more than karma; our relationships also play an important role in the construction of the soul.

Next, consider our emotions. Emotions are just recycled energy. Emotions do not originate with us. They come and go depending on situations, circumstances, relationships, and events. On September 11, 2001, the date of the World Trade Center disaster, fear and terror were common emotions, triggered by the events of that day. Those powerful emotions continued for months. Emotions are never created in isolation; they always come about because of some interaction with the environment. In the absence of circumstances or relationships, there is no emotion. So even though I may fly into a rage, it is not actually *my* anger. It is anger that has settled on me for the moment.

Each emotion is dependent on the context, circumstances, and relationships that define your reality at that moment.

And what about our thoughts? Well, our thoughts are recycled information. Every thought we have is actually part of a collective database. One hundred years ago it would have been impossible to say, "I'm going to Disney World on Delta Air Lines." There was no concept of those things in the world at large; therefore I could not have that thought. All but the most original thoughts are simply recycled information, and even the most original thoughts are actually quantum leaps of creativity that occur from that same collective, recycled bed of information.

Although the phrase "quantum leap" has become common in everyday conversation, it actually has a very specific meaning. When we are taught about atoms in school, we are usually told that there is a nucleus that contains protons and neutrons, and that electrons circle the nucleus in fixed orbits or shells that are varying distances from the nucleus.

Sodium atom (Na)

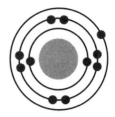

We are told that electrons stay in one particular orbit, but sometimes change to a different orbit. If it absorbs energy, an electron can jump to a higher orbit; if it releases energy, it can drop to a lower orbit. What most of us are never told is that when an electron changes orbits, it does not move through space to arrive at its new location; rather, at one moment the electron is in orbit A, and in the very next moment it is in orbit B, without having traveled through the space in between. This is what is meant by a quantum leap. A quantum leap is a change in status from one set of circumstances to another set of circumstances that takes place immediately, without passing through the circumstances in between.

Scientists have learned that they cannot predict when and where a quantum leap will occur. They can create mathematical models that allow them to estimate the quantum leaps, but they are never totally predictable.

Scientists recognize the unpredictability of nature, and have been trying to make sense of it.

The new science of chaos is attempting to predict the unpredictable through intricate mathematical models. In the classic example, a butterfly flutters its wings in Texas and there is a typhoon in Tokyo six days later. The connection may not seem obvious, but it exists. That little change of air pressure caused by the butterfly can get multiplied and magnified, resulting in a tornado. But it can never be entirely predicted. That's why weather forecasters seem to be wrong so often, and why any forecast longer than about forty-eight hours away is unreliable. Yet among all the possible occurrences in the world, weather is more predictable than just about anything else.

What this says on a spiritual level is that we can never really know what direction life will take, what changes those small butterfly-flutters of intention and action might cause in our destiny. And at the same time, it also tells us that we can never truly know the mind of God. We can never fully understand the how, where, and when of anything, even something as simple as boiling water. We have to surrender to uncertainty, while appreciating its intricate beauty.

All creativity is based on quantum leaps and uncertainty. At particular moments in time, truly novel ideas emanate from the collective bed of information. These ideas did not originate in the fortunate individual, but in the collective consciousness. This is why significant scientific discoveries are often made by two or more different people at the same time. The ideas are already circulating in the collective unconscious, and prepared minds are ready to translate that information. This is the nature of genius, to be able to grasp the knowable even when no one else recognizes that it is present. At any given moment, the innovation or creative idea doesn't exist, and in the next moment, it is part of our conscious world. In between, where was it? It came from the virtual domain, at the level of the universal spirit, where everything is potential. Sometimes this potential creates something predictable, sometimes it creates something novel, but in this realm all possibilities already exist.

So now we may ask, if my body, emotions, thoughts, and personality are not original or created by me, who am I really? According to many of the great spiritual traditions, one of the great truths is that "I am the other." Without the other, we would not exist. Your soul is the reflection of all souls. Imagine trying to understand the complex web of personal interactions that have made you who you are today—all your family and friends, every teacher and classmate you've ever had, every shop clerk in every store you've ever visited, everyone you've ever worked with or come in contact with at any point in your life. And then, in order to understand all those people and the type of influence they may have had on you, you have to find out who *they* are. So now you have to describe the web of relationships surrounding every one of those people who form your relationship network. Eventually, you would find that you would need to describe the whole universe in order to define a single person. In truth, then, every single person *is* the whole universe. You are the infinite, seen from a specific, localized point of view. Your soul is the part of you that is universal and individual at the same time, and it is a reflection of all other souls.

To define the soul in this way, therefore, is to understand that your soul is both personal and universal at the same time, which has meaning and implications beyond your personal experience of life. The soul is the observer who interprets and makes choices in a confluence of relationships. These relationships provide the background, setting, characters, and events that shape the stories of our lives. Just as the soul is created through relationships and is a reflection of all relationships, the experience of life is created from context and meaning.

By *context* I mean everything that surrounds us that allows us to understand the meaning of individual actions, words, occurrences, or anything else. A word, for example, can have different meanings depending on what surrounds it, or its context. If I say the word "bark" without context, you won't know whether I mean the bark of a dog or the bark of a tree. When we say that someone took our words "out of context," we know that the meaning of our words was misunderstood, because context determines the meaning of everything. The flow of meaning is the flow of life. Our context determines how we will interpret what we encounter in life, and these interpretations become our experience.

Finally, we come to a more complete definition of a soul. *A soul is the observer who interprets and makes choices based on karma; it is also a confluence of relationships, out of which emerge contexts and meaning, and it is this flow of context and meaning that creates experience.* So it is through the soul that we create our lives.

Our stories are derived from relationships, contexts, and meanings triggered through memory, arising from karma and experience. As we live out these stories, we start to realize that they are not original.

Although the details of the stories vary from individual to individual, the themes and motifs are timeless, basic archetypes that replay endlessly: heroes and villains; sin and redemption; the divine and the diabolical; forbidden lust and unconditional love. These are the same themes that keep many of us fascinated by soap operas, gossip columns, and tabloids, where we see them expressed in slightly exaggerated form. We're fascinated because we can identify some aspect of our souls in those stories. These are the same archetypes that are represented in exaggerated form in mythologies, so whether we examine Indian mythology or Greek mythology or Egyptian mythology, we find these same themes and motifs. The drama of these stories is more compelling and more dramatic than fiction because they resonate in our soul.

So now we can refine our definition of the soul even further. *The soul is the confluence of meanings, contexts, relationships, and mythical stories or archetypal themes that give rise to everyday thoughts, memories, and desires (conditioned by karma) that create the stories in which we participate.*

In nearly everyone, this participation in the stories of our lives is happening automatically, without awareness. We live like actors in a play who are given only one line at a time, going through the motions without understanding the full story. But when you get in touch with your soul, you see the whole script for the drama. You understand. You still participate in the story, but now you participate joyously, consciously, and fully. You can make choices based on knowledge and born out of freedom. Each moment takes on a deeper quality that comes from appreciation of what it means in the context of your life.

What is even more thrilling is that we, ourselves, are capable of rewriting the play or changing our roles by applying intention, grasping the opportunities that arise from coincidence, and being true to the calling of our souls.

4

INTENTION

EVERYTHING THAT HAPPENS IN THE UNIVERSE starts with intention. This intention always arises in the nonlocal or universal mind, but it localizes through the individual mind. And having localized, it becomes physical reality.

In fact, physical reality would not exist were it not for intent. Intent activates nonlocal, synchronized correlation in the brain. Whenever there is cognition or perception of physical reality, the brain's disparate regions show a "phase and frequency locking in" of the firing patterns of individual neurons in different parts of the brain. This is nonlocal synchronization around a frequency of forty hertz (forty cycles per second). This synchronization, also called binding, is a requirement for cognition. Without it you would not see a person as a person, a house as a house, a tree as a tree, or a face in a photograph as a face. You might just observe dots of black and white, scattered lines, patches of light and dark. In fact, the objects of your perception register only as on-off electromagnetic signals in your brain. Synchronization organized by intent converts dots and spots, scattered lines, electrical discharges, patterns of light and darkness, into a wholeness, a gestalt that creates a picture of the world as a subjective experience. The world does not exist as pictures, but only as these patches of on-off impulses, these dots and spots, these digital codes of seemingly random electrical firings. Synchronization through intent organizes them into an experience in the brain—a sound, a texture, a form, a taste, and a smell. You as nonlocal intelligence "label" that experience and suddenly there is the creation of a material object in subjective consciousness.

All learning, remembering, reasoning, drawing of inferences, and motor activity are preceded by intent. Intent is the very basis of creation.

The ancient Vedic texts known as the Upanishads declare, "You are what your deepest desire is. As is your desire, so is your intention. As is your intention, so is your will. As is your will, so is your deed. As is your deed, so is your destiny." Our destiny ultimately comes from the deepest level of desire and also from the deepest level of intention. The two are intimately linked to each other.

What *is* intention? Most people say it's a thought of something that you want to accomplish in your life or that you want for yourself. But really it is more than that. An intention is a way of fulfilling a certain need that you have, whether that need is for material things, for a relationship, for spiritual fulfillment, or for love. Intention is a thought that you have that will help you to fulfill a need. And the logic is that once you fulfill that need, you will be happy.

Seen this way, the goal of all our intentions is to be happy or fulfilled. So we can see that the ultimate goal of all goals is a fulfillment at the spiritual level that we call happiness or joy or love.

When intention is repeated, that creates habit. The more an intention is repeated, the more likely it is that the universal consciousness will create the same pattern and manifest the intention in the physical world.

Only with repeated thoughts can the impossible be made possible through the intention of the nonlocal mind.

The nonlocal mind in you is the same as the nonlocal mind in me, or, in fact, in a rhinoceros or in a giraffe or in a bird or in a worm. This nonlocal mind, this pure consciousness, is what gives us the sense of

"I," the "I" that says "I am Deepak," the "I" that says "I'm a bird," the "I" that says who you are or who you believe you are. This universal consciousness is the only "I" there is. But that single, universal "I" differentiates; it morphs itself into an almost infinite number of observers and observed, seers and scenery, organic forms and inorganic forms—all the beings and objects that make up the physical world. So, before the "I am" says "I am Deepak," or a giraffe, or a worm, it is simply "I am." The infinite creative potential of the "I" organizes the communal "I" into the "I" that is you, or me, or any other thing in the universe.

This is the same concept as the two levels of the soul, the universal soul and the individual soul, but put into a personal context. As human beings, we are used to thinking of our individual selves as "I," without noticing or appreciating the greater, universal "I" that is also called the universal soul. The use of the word "I" is merely a clever reference point we use for locating our unique point of view within the universal soul. But when we define ourselves solely as an individual "I," we lose the ability to imagine beyond the boundaries of what is traditionally considered possible. In the universal "I," everything is not only possible, it already exists, and simply requires intent to collapse it into a reality in the physical world.

The difference between local mind and nonlocal mind is the difference between ordinary and extraordinary. The local mind is personal and individual to each of us. It holds our ego, the self-defined "I" that wanders through the world a slave to our conditioned habits. By its very nature, the local mind separates us from the rest of creation.

Nonlocal mind, on the other hand, is pure soul or spirit, known as universal consciousness. Operating outside the boundaries of normal space and time, it is the great organizing and unifying force in the universe, infinite in scope and duration. It allows us to imagine beyond the boundaries of what local mind sees as "possible," to think "outside the box," and to believe in miracles.

Intention always originates in the universal domain. Ultimately, it is universal intention that fulfills the local intention, as long as it serves the needs of the local mind (me) and the nonlocal mind (the universal spirit). Only then will both local and nonlocal minds cooperate. But there is a confounding factor at play. There are billions of human beings and trillions of other entities on earth, all with local intentions.

At every location, every organism could be thinking "It's my intent!" Each and every one believes it is their personal local "I" that is doing something, but in the larger scheme, all these different local minds are actually co-arising and co-creating each other, through the intent of the nonlocal mind. The trees must breathe so I can breathe. The rivers must flow so that my blood can circulate. In the end, there's only one exuberant, abundant, eternal, rhythmic, inseparable "I." All separation is illusion.

We are so attached to our local, individual, personal "I" that we are blinded to the magnificence that lies beyond it. Ignorance is constricted awareness. In order to notice something, you have to ignore everything else. That's how nonlocal becomes local. When I notice anything, I ignore everything else around it, which nevertheless contributes to its existence and is therefore a part of it. When the "I" that is my ego observes, it observes only the particular and ignores the universal. But when "I" the spirit sees, it sees the flow of the universe that makes the particular possible.

Intention orchestrates infinite possibilities. You might wonder what kind of intent is ideal. What would you ask if your intention could be fulfilled right now?

For every intention, we might well ask, "How would this serve me and how would it serve everybody I come into contact with?" And if the answer is that it will create true joy and fulfillment in me and all those affected by my actions, then my intention, together with surrender to the nonlocal mind, orchestrates its own fulfillment.

Remember, your thoughts must not conflict with the designs of the universe. Wishing to win the lottery can magnify your sense of separation from the universe. Frequently lottery winners report alienation from friends and family and no greater happiness. When money alone becomes the goal, it alienates you.

How do you know which of your intentions is likely to be fulfilled? The answer lies in paying attention to the clues provided by the nonlocal mind. Notice the coincidences in your life. Coincidences are messages. They are clues from God or spirit or nonlocal reality, urging you to break out of your karmic conditioning, your familiar patterns of thinking. They are offering you an opportunity to enter a domain of awareness where you feel loved and cared for by the infinite intelligence that is your source. Spiritual traditions call this the state of grace.

5

THE ROLE OF COINCIDENCE

To talk about coincidences as coded messages from the nonlocal intelligence makes life sound like a mystery novel. Pay attention, watch for clues, decipher their meanings, and eventually the truth will be revealed. In many ways, that's exactly what happens. After all, life is the ultimate mystery.

What makes life mysterious is that our destiny seems hidden from us, and only at the end of our lives will we be in a position to look back and see the path we followed. In retrospect, the narrative of our lives appears perfectly logical. We can easily follow the thread of continuity upon which we gathered our life's experiences. Even now, at whatever point you are in your life, look back and notice how naturally your life flowed from one milestone to the next, from one place or job to another, from one set of circumstances to an entirely different set. Notice how effortless it all could have been if you had only known where your path was leading. Most people look back and ask, What was I so worried about? Why was I so hard on myself, or on my children?

If we were able to live at the level of the soul all the time, there would be no need for hindsight to appreciate the great truths of life. We would know them in advance. We would participate in creating the adventures of our lives. The path would be clearly marked, and we would need no signposts, no clues, and no coincidences.

Most of us don't live at the level of the soul, however, so we must depend on coincidences to show us the will of the universe. We have all experienced coincidences in our lives. The word itself perfectly describes its meaning: *co* means "with," and *incidence* means "event." So the word *coincidence* refers to events or incidents that occur *with* other incidents—two or more events occurring at the same time. Because the experience of coincidences is universal, most people take them for granted, life's little quirky moments that we marvel over, then quickly forget.

Coincidences are so much more than amusements. A coincidence is a clue to the intention of the universal spirit, and as such it is rich with significance.

What *is* the meaning in a coincidence? The deeper part of you already knows, but that awareness has to be brought to the surface. The meaning does not come from the coincidence itself. It comes from you, the person who is having the experience.

Having an intention is easy; it's as simple as making a wish for one's life. Becoming more spiritual is difficult. Many people who believe themselves to be spiritual are still not tapping into the vast ocean of the spirit force. Rather, they swim across the surface of that ocean, never diving to discover the depths of the universal experience.

MIRACLES IN THE REAL WORLD

Miracles are real phenomena. Every tradition addresses the existence of miracles, but they all use different language. We label events as miracles when a desired outcome manifests in a dramatic fashion: We want to be healed from a terrible illness, or attain material wealth, or find our purpose. Then when these events occur, we say, how miraculous! Someone has an intention or a desire or a thought, and then it happens. A miracle, then, is a very dramatic example of what happens when a person is able to tap into the spiritual domain and apply intention to manifest their destiny.

Let me give you an example of a remarkable coincidence. David was in love with a woman named Joanna. He was utterly in love, but a little tentative about commitment and marriage. He finally decided that he would take Joanna to a park and propose to her. He was still leery of commitment, but when he awoke that morning he felt overcome by a feeling of peace, a sense that all would be well. David set out the picnic blanket and was just getting up the nerve to pop the question when a plane flew overhead trailing an advertising banner. Joanna looked up and said, "I wonder what that banner says." Without thinking David blurted out, "The banner says, 'Joanna, marry me.' " They both looked more closely, and there indeed was a banner that read, JOANNA, MARRY ME. She fell into his arms, they kissed, and at that moment David knew that marrying her was exactly right for him. The next day, they read in the local newspaper that someone else had proposed to his girlfriend,

Joanna, with a banner over the park; the plane just happened to be overhead at exactly the right moment for David. This remarkable coincidence was a clue to David's future, a miracle. The two remain happily married to this day.

When you begin seeing coincidences as life opportunities, every coincidence becomes meaningful. Every coincidence becomes an opportunity for creativity. Every coincidence becomes an opportunity for you to become the person the universe intended you to be.

This is the ultimate truth of synchrodestiny—that the sum total of the universe is conspiring to create your personal destiny. To do so it uses "*acausal* nonlocal connections." What are acausal connections? If we look at all the disparate incidents in our lives very deeply, they all have a history woven together with a personal destiny. *Acausal* means that the incidents are connected to each other, yet without a direct cause-and-effect relationship, at least on the surface. They are *acausal*, from a Latin phrase meaning "without cause."

We cannot even imagine the complex forces behind every event that occurs in our lives. There's a conspiracy of coincidences that weaves the web of karma or destiny and creates an individual's personal life—mine, or yours. The only reason we don't experience synchronicity in our daily lives is that we do not live from the level where it is happening. Usually we see only cause-and-effect relationships: Yet beneath the surface, something else is happening. Invisible to us is a whole web of connections. As it becomes apparent, we see how our intentions are woven into this web, which is much more context-bound, much more relational, much more holistic, much more nurturing than our surface experience.

According to a poem by Rumi, one of my favorite poets and philosophers, "This is not the real reality. The real reality is behind the curtain. In truth, we are not here. This is our shadow." What we experience as everyday reality is merely a shadow play. Behind the curtain there is a soul, living and dynamic and immortal, beyond the reach of space and time. By acting from that level, we can consciously influence our destiny. This happens through the *synchro*nization of seemingly *acausal* relationships to mold a *destiny*—hence, synchrodestiny. In synchrodestiny, we consciously participate in the creation of our lives by understanding the world that is beyond our senses, the world of the soul.

THE COINCIDENCE OF
THE UNIVERSE

Nothing—absolutely nothing—would exist were it not for a remarkable set of coincidences. I once read an article by a physicist describing the Big Bang that gave birth to our universe. In that moment, the number of particles created was slightly more than the number of antiparticles. The particles and the antiparticles then collided and annihilated each other, filling the universe with photons. Because of the initial imbalance, there were a few particles left after the annihilation and these created what we know as the material world. You and I and the rest of the universe, including all the stars and galaxies, are leftover stuff from the moment of creation. The total number of particles left over was 10^{80} (that's the number 1 followed by 80 zeros). If the number of particles had been even slightly greater, gravitational forces would have forced the young universe to collapse on itself, forming one huge black hole, which would mean no you, no me, no stars, or galaxies. If the number of matter-particles had been even slightly smaller, the universe would have expanded so fast that there would have been no time for the galaxies to form as they did.

The development of carbon and oxygen, essential for the creation of biological organisms, required many coincidences to occur and to continue to occur from the moment of the Big Bang. That you and I exist, and that the universe with its stars, galaxies, and planets exists, is a highly improbable event! A total coincidence! A miracle, tracking back to the birth of time.

ATTENTION AND INTENTION

Consciousness orchestrates its activity in response to both attention and intention. Whatever you put your attention on becomes energized. Whatever you take your attention away from dwindles. On the other hand, intention is the key to transformation, as we have seen. So you could say that attention activates the energy field, and intention activates the information field, which causes transformation.

In the physical world, we have many different ways of acquiring information: newspapers, books, television, radio, cell phone conversations, shortwave radios—all these ways of tapping into various kinds of information, and many more, are readily available to us. You can simply tune in to them with your sensory apparatus—look, listen, feel, smell, taste the environment around you. But if you want to tap in to the information at the level of the soul, you need a different way to get the information.

We don't normally have our attention in that unseen dimension, but everything that's happening in the visible world has its roots there. Everything is connected with everything else. In the spiritual world, those connections become visible. But in the physical world, we only glimpse the connections in the clues given to us through coincidence. As our attention creates energy, intention brings about the transformation of that energy. Attention and intention are the most powerful tools of the spiritually adept. They are the triggers for attracting both a certain kind of energy and a certain kind of information.

So the more attention you put on coincidences, the more you attract other coincidences, which will help you clarify their meaning. Putting your attention on the coincidence attracts the energy, and then asking the question "What does it mean?" attracts the information. The answer might come as a certain insight, or intuitive feeling, or an encounter, or a new relationship. You may experience four seemingly unrelated coincidences, then watch the evening news and have an insight. Ah-ha! That's what they meant for me! The more attention you put on coincidences and the more you inquire into their significance, the more often the coincidences occur and the more clearly their meaning comes into view. Once you can see and interpret the coincidences, your path to fulfillment emerges.

In most people's experience, the past resides only in memory and the future resides only in imagination. But at the spiritual level, the past and the future and all the different probabilities of life exist simultaneously. Everything is happening all at once.

NURTURING COINCIDENCE

Now we know that putting your attention on coincidences attracts more coincidences, and applying intention reveals their meaning. In this way coincidences become clues to the will of the universe, providing a way for us to see its synchronicity and take advantage of life's boundless opportunities.

People who are sensitive to events and stimuli around them will be sensitive to coincidences sent from the universe. Clues may be as subtle as the smell of pipe smoke wafting through an open window, which makes you think of your father, which reminds you of a book he loved, which then somehow comes to play an important role in your life at the moment.

When a coincidence arises, don't ignore it. Ask yourself, What is the message here? What is the significance of this? You don't need to go digging for the answers. Ask the question, and the answers will emerge. They may arrive as a sudden insight, a spontaneous creative experience, or they may be something very different. Perhaps you will meet a person who is somehow related to the coincidence that occurred. An encounter, a relationship, a chance meeting, a situation, a circumstance will immediately give you a clue to its meaning. "Oh, so that's what it was all about!"

Another thing you can do to nurture coincidence is to keep a diary or journal of coincidences in your life. After years of note-taking, I classify coincidences as tiny, medium, whoppers, and double-whoppers. You can do this in any way that is easy for you. For some people, it is easiest to maintain a daily journal and underline or highlight words or phrases or names of things that show up as coincidences. Other people keep a special coincidence diary. They start a new page for each significant coincidence, then jot down any other connections to that event on its page.

So remain sensitive, observe coincidences during

both your daytime living and your nighttime dreaming, and pay special attention to anything that breaks the probability amplitude—the statistical likelihood of a space-time event.

Of course, life can be difficult, and we each have daily chores, responsibilities, and obligations that can become overwhelming. Coincidences may come flying at you from all directions, or they may seem to dry up entirely. How do you find your way in such a complex world? Take five minutes every day and just sit in silence. In that time, put these questions to your attention and heart: "Who am I? What do I want for my life? What do I want from my life today?" Then let go, and let your stream of consciousness, your quieter inner voice, supply the answers. Then, after five minutes, write them down. Do this every day and you'll be surprised at how situations, circumstances, events, and people will orchestrate themselves around the answers. This is the beginning of synchrodestiny.

For some people, answering those questions for the first time can be difficult. Many of us are not used to thinking in terms of our own wants and needs, and if we do, we certainly don't expect to fulfill them. If you haven't defined your life's goal for yourself, what do you do then? It would be helpful if the universe would give us one big clue, or a giant compass, if you will, pointing to the direction we should be taking. In fact, the compass is there. To find it, you need only look inside yourself to discover your soul's purest desire, its dream for your life. Sit quietly. Once you reveal this desire and understand its essential nature, then you have a constant beacon, which we can make manifest in the form of archetypal symbols.

6

DESIRES AND ARCHETYPES

WE COME NOW TO THE HEART OF SYNCHRODES-
tiny. We have discovered the dual nature of the soul,
and we understand that we are fully part of the nonlocal intelligence, just as a wave is part of the ocean. We
have learned to see the synchronicity in all things, the
matrix that links us to the source of the universe. We
have learned to value coincidences as messages from
the nonlocal intelligence that point us in the direction of our destiny, and we know that our intentions
can influence this direction. All these revelations are
essential for living a fulfilled life. But when we look
for guidance in how to construct our everyday lives,
we still need to answer the central question of self:
What are my dreams and desires? And that can only

be answered by asking, in addition, Who am I? What do I want? What's my purpose in this lifetime?

We know that our deepest relationships and meanings and contexts derive from the soul. And our aspiration, that grand and wonderful and mythical thing that we yearn to do, also ultimately derives from the soul. In our time here on earth, this individual soul will not be fulfilled unless it completes its mythical quest, which we can think of as the Grand Plan around which our destinies are organized. Inside every human being there is an overarching theme, a template for heroic living, a god or a goddess in embryo that yearns to be born. This is who we were meant to be, the self that we deny ourselves because most of us cannot see the field of limitless potential that is open to us. This is our best self, the egoless self, that bit of the universe acting through us for the good of all.

People who live ordinary, mundane lives have not gotten in touch with the mythical being inside them. You can pave the path to enlightenment by understanding the plan written on your soul, by nurturing the relationships that give you context and meanings, and by enacting your mythical drama. Out of that is born love and compassion. Out of that comes fulfillment and completion.

These mythical stories, these heroes and heroines within, are called archetypes. Archetypes are perennial themes that reside at the level of the collective, universal soul. These themes are representations of our collective soul's yearnings, imagination, and deepest desires. These themes have existed forever. We see them in the writings of ancient cultures, in literature throughout the ages. Their shapes shift depending on where we are in history, but their core remains the same.

Archetypes are born of the collective soul, but they are enacted by individual souls. Their mythical dramas play out daily in our physical world. We can see Robert Downey Jr. as the embodiment of Dionysus or Bacchus, the untamed, fun-loving spirit. Princess Diana was Artemis, the nonconformist, the wild one, the rule breaker, the fearless warrior who fights for what she believes.

Every human being is attuned to some archetype, or two or three archetypes. Every one of us is hardwired at the level of the soul to enact or model archetypal characteristics. The activation of an archetype releases its patterning forces that allow us to become more of what we already are destined to be. And our individual archetypes are reflected in our desires or intentions. So, who are you? What do you want? What is the purpose of your existence? At the deepest level these questions are asked of the soul. And to find the answers you must speak to that part of the soul that is unique to you. And as we do, we learn to define our individual archetypes.

We live in a society that is so totally goal oriented that everything has to have a label, but this is less helpful when you explore the nature of your soul. If you label yourself, you become stuck, like a butterfly caught in a jar. Adopting an archetype is not labeling because it is not about limitations. Quite the opposite. Archetypes are life models, images and ideas that guide the direction of your life toward your soul's ultimate destiny. Recognizing your true nature and allowing it to blossom is part of the beauty of living from the level of the soul—you become the hero or heroine of a mythical saga.

You can begin to know your own archetypes and your own destiny only by accessing the will of the universal soul, by looking deep inside and defining your innermost desires, by choosing the archetype that most closely matches your intentions, and following its ancient pattern.

THE PURPOSE OF ARCHETYPES

Discovering archetypes is a highly personal experience. No one can look at you, even if they know you well, and tell you, "Oh, you are this archetype." Vedic science, the ancient wisdom tradition of India, says that unless you can get in touch with that embryo of a god or goddess incubating inside you, unless you can let that embryo be fully born, then your life will always be mundane. But once that god or goddess expresses itself through you, then you will do grand and wondrous things.

Archetypes are vital to understanding and defining who we are, individual expressions of a collective consciousness. Mythology is the wellspring of our civilization. Whenever somebody does anything remarkable—when astronauts walk on the moon, when a pilot embarks on the first solo flight across the Atlantic—these are mythical quests, Jason in search of the Golden Fleece, Icarus soaring in his wings of feathers and wax. From Persephone's abduction by Pluto to Orpheus seeking his bride among the shades of Hades, to Apollo, Krishna, and all the stories of Celtic mythology—this is the deepest wellspring of civilization and identity.

Archetypes are enacted by people like Mahatma Gandhi, Martin Luther King Jr., Rosa Parks, anyone who reaches beyond daily life into the realm of the wondrous. They are able to achieve greatness because they tapped into the collective consciousness, which gave them the ability to see several event lines simultaneously and predict the future based on choices in the moment. They say that when Mahatma Gandhi was thrown out of the train in Durban, South Africa, he closed his eyes and saw the British Empire crumbling halfway across the world. That one episode changed the course of history.

FINDING YOUR ARCHETYPES

The process of finding an archetype should be joyous. Don't worry about choosing unwisely. Because archetypes spring from the collective consciousness, every archetype is present in every one of us. But some archetypes are represented more strongly. Your goal is to find the one, two, or even three archetypes that resonate with you most powerfully, those that represent your heart. Do not choose who you wish to be, or even which qualities you most admire, but seek out the qualities that you feel drawn to, that motivate you, that inspire you. You will know them when you find them. Best of all, there are no wrong answers.

Write down your three symbols or archetypes. Then, begin to collect artwork or pictures or symbols or jewelry that remind you of this archetype. Some people create a small altar for their archetypes as a place to center the search for self. If the principal qualities of your archetypes can be expressed in words or phrases, write them on a piece of paper so that you have something to remind you of them. At least once a day, preferably after meditation, look at these reminders and silently issue them an invitation: "Please come and express yourself through me." Let them be a reminder of your life's inspiration. When you feel lost or distracted in the world, they will be your compass back to your true self.

part two

PAVING
DESTINY'S
PATH

7

MEDITATION AND MANTRAS

THE MOST POWERFUL TOOL WE HAVE FOR LEARN-ing to live synchrodestiny, to see the connective patterns of the universe, to make miracles out of our desires, is meditation. Meditation allows us to place our attention and intention in these more subtle planes, giving us access to all that unseen, untapped information and energy.

If your doctor gave you a prescription to walk for twenty minutes twice a day, and told you that those walks alone would lead to good health, peace of mind, freedom from worry, increased success in your personal and professional life, would you follow her recommendation? Most people would at least give it a try. The synchrodestiny prescription is to meditate for fifteen to twenty minutes twice a day, followed by a

moment of extending an invitation to your archetypes. If you do that twice a day, you'll start to see a
transformation in your life. Beyond that, conduct
yourself just as you always have before. Meditate in
the morning, live the rest of your day, and then meditate again in the evening. That alone will start you on
the road to transforming your life and creating the
miracles you want.

Meditation is a simple process that is difficult to
describe, but is very easy to do once you begin to
practice it regularly. Here I will present the basics of
meditation so that you can successfully apply the
principles of synchrodestiny described in the rest of
the book.

HOW TO MEDITATE

Our minds are constantly active, always jumping
from thought to thought, emotion to emotion. Getting in touch with the nonlocal intelligence, the universal soul that lies within us and is part of us all,
requires finding a way past the fog of distracting
thoughts that typically hide it from us. We cannot
fight our way through that barrier any more than we
can fight our way through a real fog. If we are quiet,

we encounter moments of pure silence—I call them thought "gaps"—and through these gaps we can glimpse the deeper level of the soul. Each glimpse increases our understanding, and eventually our consciousness becomes expanded.

The purpose of meditation is to stop thinking for a time, wait for the fog of thought to thin, and glimpse the spirit within. Controlling the flood of thoughts is very difficult for most people. Beginners can sometimes become very frustrated, but frustration is just another thought, another emotion that gets in the way. The goal is to release all thoughts, quietly, passively.

A common way to begin meditation is to gently focus on one thing so that it becomes more difficult for stray thoughts to enter your mind. I like to start with a breathing meditation.

To begin meditation, find a comfortable position. Sit in a comfortable chair, with your feet flat on the ground. Place your hands in your lap with the palms facing upward. Close your eyes and begin witnessing your breath. Observe the inflow and outflow of your breath without attempting to control it in any way. You may find that your breathing spontaneously gets faster or slower, deeper or shallower, and may even pause for a time. Observe the changes without resistance or anticipation. Whenever your attention drifts away from your breath to a sound in the environment, or a sensation in your body, or a thought in your mind, gently return your awareness to your breathing.

This is the basic meditation. Once a person becomes comfortable with simply sitting quietly and focusing on breathing, I recommend adding a mantra, which creates a mental environment that will allow you to expand your consciousness.

MANTRAS

The word *mantra* has two components to it: *man,* which is the root sound of the word *mind,* and *tra,* which is the root sound of the word *instrument.* So, the word *mantra* literally means an instrument of the mind. The ancient wisdom tradition of Vedanta examined the various sounds produced in nature, the fundamental vibrations of the world around us. According to Vedanta, these sounds are an expression of the infinite or cosmic mind, and provide the basis for every human language.

We know that the manifest universe—which appears to be made up of solid objects—is actually made up of vibrations, with different objects vibrating at different frequencies.

The ancient seers are said to have heard these vibrations of the universe when they were in deep meditation. We can all hear these same vibrations any time. It is very simple. If you quiet your mind and sit silently, you will hear vibrations. You can try it any time you want.

The Vedas also maintain that if you recite a mantra out loud, its special pattern of vibrations creates its own effects, and can create events in our current physical realm. Reciting the mantra mentally creates a mental vibration, which then becomes more abstract.

The mantra I use, and that I recommend for achieving synchrodestiny, is the simple mantra "so-hum." This is the mantra of the breath; if you observe your breathing you'll hear "so-hum" as air moves in and out of your lungs. As you inhale, the sound of that vibration is "so." And as you exhale, the sound becomes "hum." If you want, you can experiment with this. Inhale deeply, close your eyes and your mouth, and exhale forcefully through your nose. If you concentrate, you'll hear the "hum" sound quite clearly.

One of the techniques of meditation is, in fact, simply focusing on where your breath comes from.

With your eyes closed, inhale and think the word "so"; on the exhale, think the word "hum." Gradually both the breath and the sound will become quieter and quieter and quieter, and the breath becomes so quiet that it almost seems to stop. By quieting your breath, you quiet your mind. When you transcend, the mantra "so-hum" entirely disappears, and your breath pauses momentarily. Time itself comes to a stop and you're in the field of pure consciousness, the nonlocal domain, spirit, the ground of being.

The mantra, then, is a way to experience nonlocal consciousness.

SUTRA

The sutra is a mantra that has meaning. The mantra itself has no meaning. It's just a vibration, a sound. It becomes a sutra when there's an intention coded in the sound. The word *sutra* is a Sanskrit word, related to the Latin noun *sutura,* which is the base of the English word *suture,* meaning "to join together by sewing." So a *sutra* is actually a stitch on the soul, and the stitch is one of intention. Both mantras and sutras allow you to transcend to a deeper consciousness.

Therefore you could use the "so-hum" mantra, for example, to transcend. Then you could use an actual word, a sutra, to embed a particular intention into your consciousness.

The messages in a sutra are simple and complex at the same time. If I say the sutra *"aham brahmasmi"* ("the core of my being is the ultimate reality, the root and ground of the universe, the source of all that exists"), it might take a whole day, or half a book, to explain and understand that one sentence. Yet the sutra contains the complete understanding of that complex thought. So this sutra, these two words, summarizes the whole understanding. By simply putting your attention on this sutra, you will experience and understand the entire explanation contained within it.

There are mantras and sutras that have been used successfully for thousands of years, and you will find them in the chapters that follow. They provide a path to synchrodestiny. Although the Sanskrit words that embody those sutras may sound foreign to you, that doesn't diminish their effectiveness. You do not even have to understand the meanings of the sutras in order for them to work. Remember, these are the sounds of nature, with meaning attached. The soul will understand their meaning even if you do not.

THE FOLLOWING CHAPTERS describe the seven Principles of Synchrodestiny and provide exercises to strengthen your understanding of them. These seven principles are ways of thinking about the qualities of nonlocal intelligence and relating them to your life. Each principle offers a new lesson, a new way of relating that brings you closer to spirit, with its infinite possibilities.

Here is the program for achieving synchrodestiny, a specific way to use all the elements I've discussed so far:

1. Begin each day by going to a quiet place where you will not be disturbed. Gather symbols of your archetypes and place them in front of you.

2. Meditate for twenty minutes using the so-hum mantra. This expands your consciousness and puts you in a receptive frame of mind.

3. Immediately upon completing the meditation, when you open your eyes, look upon the symbols of your archetypes and invite or invoke the archetypal energies to express themselves through you. Say, "I ask that you become part of me and work through me. Guide me through my life."

4. Read the synchrodestiny principle for this day. There are seven Principles of Synchrodestiny and

seven days of the week. On the day you begin, read the first principle. You don't have to understand every concept contained in that principle. Just read it. On the second day, move on to the second principle. On the third day, move on to the third principle, and so on. I recommend that you don't skip around; the principles are arranged in an order that builds, one upon the other. On the eighth day, go back to the first principle and start the series over again.

Each principle has a sutra that encapsulates the teachings of the principle. Thoroughly understand the meaning of the sutra. Perform the exercises associated with the sutra until they have become part of your reality. After many weeks, you will be able to read the sutra alone and gain the benefit of the entire chapter.

These first four steps should take no longer than twenty or thirty minutes. Repeat the process at night.

For the rest of the day, you do not need to do anything special. Just live your life the way you normally would. The morning meditation focuses your intention for the day, even when you are not even thinking about it. By reading the principle, you create that intention, and then allow nonlocal intelligence to synchronize all the millions of individual events that need to occur to have the intention be fulfilled. That's all you need to do.

At the end of each chapter you will find one or more exercises designed to help illustrate the principles and guide you to a deeper understanding of the sutras. These are not part of the daily meditation, but a supplement. Try them whenever you feel you would like to take that extra step toward understanding the Principles of Synchrodestiny.

In the end, that's really all you need in order to reach the place where synchrodestiny happens—the seven principles, the seven sutras, your archetypes, an ability to meditate using the "so-hum" mantra, and the Sutra Statements to read when you feel yourself beginning to lose your center. In your hands these are the tools that make miracles happen.

8

THE FIRST PRINCIPLE:
YOU ARE A RIPPLE IN THE
FABRIC OF THE COSMOS

SUTRA: Aham Brahmasmi (*ah-HUM brah-MAHS-mee*)
The core of my being is the ultimate reality, the root and
ground of the universe, the source of all that exists.

THE FIRST PRINCIPLE OF SYNCHRODESTINY AC-
knowledges the underlying intelligence that gives
rise to my body, your body, and the universe as a
whole—everything from stars and galaxies to subatomic particles. This conscious intelligence field is
the wellspring of the cosmos. It is the extended body
we all share; it connects us all. The core of my being is
also the core of your being, and the core of all beings.

You and I and the universe are the same. And

when you realize that the intentions and desires that arise in you are the very intentions of the universe, you can relinquish your desire for control and let the miraculous life you were born to lead unfold in all its unimaginable magnificence.

Once you understand this premise, you will understand the sutra of the first principle of synchrodestiny: The core of my being is the ultimate reality, the root and ground of the universe, the source of all that exists. As simple as this sounds, its depth can take a lifetime to plumb, and its meaning for our lives is profound. When we fully understand this simple sutra, everything becomes possible because everything already exists within us. You and I are the same, and each of us is the infinite being projecting a particular point of view—your point of view and my point of view. My self is inseparable from all that exists, just as your self is inseparable from all that exists.

The power in this thought emerges when we realize that the self functions synchronistically. Because I am an extension of the conscious intelligence, and the conscious intelligence is the source of all reality, then I am the source of all reality. I create my own experience.

Exercise 1

THE SILENT WITNESS

Go to a quiet place where you are not likely to be disturbed. Put on a tape or CD of your favorite soothing music. Close your eyes. As you do so, turn your attention to who is really listening. Begin to notice two different facets of yourself. Your ears pick up the sound and your brain processes the notes, but that's only the mechanics of hearing. Who connects the notes so that they form music? As you are *thinking* about listening, who is doing the actual listening?

Notice the silent witness, the silent listener who is always present. This presence exists not only in yourself, but also in the space around you. It is that part of yourself that is beyond the thoughts and feelings of the moment, the part that never tires and never sleeps. Nor can this part of you ever be destroyed. Recognize that this silent witness is always there. It is that part of you that can be glimpsed when the chatter of your thoughts is silenced by meditation. Can you feel this deeper current of consciousness within you?

Awareness of this silent witness is the beginning of awareness of the conscious intelligence field—the source of all the synchronicities in our lives.

Exercise 2

WHY ARE YOU HERE?

For this exercise you will need paper and pen, and ten minutes of uninterrupted time.

Ask yourself, Why am I here? Write down the first thing that comes to mind. This question is open to many interpretations, so jot down whatever thoughts it triggers.

Then pose the question again: Why am I here? Write down a new response. Do this twenty times.

Now look over your responses. What do they tell you? Do you see any pattern or progression in the answers? What does this tell you about how you see your life?

You can see your life as a series of external and internal events, but you can also learn to see those events as connected with each other and with something more spiritual. When you do that, you will begin to see your life as an opportunity to share the special gift you alone can bestow upon the world. That's one answer to the question of why you are here. Having this kind of clarity of purpose will help you focus your intentions.

9

THE SECOND PRINCIPLE: THROUGH THE MIRROR OF RELATIONSHIPS I DISCOVER MY NONLOCAL SELF

SUTRA: Tat Tvam Asi (*taht t'vahm AH-see*)
I see the other in myself and myself in others.

UNDERSTANDING HOW HUMAN RELATIONSHIPS work is one of the most important keys to synchrodestiny. In the West, we tend to rely on popular psychology to come up with strategies for managing our thoughts and feelings. All too often self-help books propose manipulating our relationships so they can become more satisfying. But creating positive human relationships is much more than a tactic: It means providing the human environment in which synchrodestiny can take place. It's absolutely fundamental, in the same way that gravity, or having air to breathe, is fundamental.

The mantra for this principle means "I am that." This principle builds on the first principle, in which we learned that we are all extensions of the universal energy field, all a single entity with different points of view. *I am that* involves looking at everything in the world, everyone else in the world, and realizing that you are looking at another version of yourself. Through the mirror of relationship I discover my nonlocal self. For this reason, nurturing relationships is the most important activity in my life. When I look around me, everything I see is an expression of myself.

Relationship, then, is a tool for spiritual evolution, with the ultimate goal of reaching unity consciousness. We are all inevitably part of the same universal consciousness, but the real breakthroughs happen when we start to recognize that connection in our daily lives.

Relationship is one of the most effective ways to access unity consciousness because we're always in relationships.

Through the mirror of relationship—all relationships—we discover extended states of awareness. Those whom we love and those whom we are repelled by are both mirrors of ourselves. Whom are we attracted to? People who have the same traits as we have, but more so. We want to be in their company because subconsciously we feel that by doing so we, too, might manifest more of those traits as well. By the same token we are repelled by people who reflect back to us traits that we deny in our own selves. So if you are having a strong negative reaction to someone, you can be sure that they possess some traits in common with you, traits that you are not willing to embrace. If you were willing to accept those qualities, then they wouldn't upset you.

The next time you're attracted to someone, ask yourself what attracted you. Is it beauty, or grace, or elegance, or influence, or power, or intelligence? Whatever it is, know that that quality is also blossoming in you. Pay attention to these feelings, and you can begin the process of becoming more fully yourself.

Of course, the same is true of people who repel you. In becoming more fully your true self, you have to understand and embrace the less attractive qualities in yourself. The essential nature of the universe is the coexistence of opposite values. You cannot be brave if you do not have a coward inside you. You cannot be generous if you do not have a tight-fisted person inside you. You cannot be virtuous unless you also contain the capacity for evil.

There's a wonderful Sufi story that illustrates how this mirror affects our lives. A man entered a village and went to see the Sufi master, the wise old man of the village. The visitor said, "I'm deciding whether I should move here or not. I'm wondering what kind of a neighborhood this is. Can you tell me about the people here?" The Sufi master said, "Tell me what kind of people lived where you came from." The visitor said, "Oh, they were highway robbers, cheats, and liars." The old Sufi master said, "You know, those are exactly the same kinds of people who live here." The visitor left the village and never came back. Half an hour later, another man entered the village. He sought out the Sufi master and said, "I'm thinking of moving here. Can you tell me what kind of people live here?" Again the Sufi master said, "Tell me what kind of people lived where you came from." The visitor said, "Oh, they were the kindest, gentlest, most compassionate, loving people. I shall miss them terribly." The Sufi master said, "Those are exactly the kinds of people who live here, too."

This story reminds us that the traits we see most clearly in others exist most strongly in our selves. To do this, we need to be comfortable with our ambiguity, to embrace all aspects of our selves. At a deep level we need to recognize that we are not flawed simply because we have negative traits. No one has only positive traits. Recognizing that we have negative traits simply means that we are complete. And in that completeness we gain greater access to our universal, nonlocal selves.

Exercise 3

EMBRACING DUALITY

For this exercise, you'll need a piece of paper and a pen.

Think about a specific person whom you find very attractive. On the left side of the paper list ten or more desirable qualities that person possesses. List anything that comes to mind. Write quickly. The secret is not to allow your conscious mind time to edit your thoughts. Why do you like this person? Why do you find him or her attractive? What do you most admire? Is that person kind, loving, flexible, independent? Do you admire that he or she drives a nice car, has a flattering hairstyle, or lives in a desirable house? You can write down as many qualities as you like, but don't stop before reaching ten.

Now switch gears and bring into your awareness somebody whom you find repulsive, someone who irritates you, annoys you, aggravates you, or makes you uncomfortable in some way. Start to define those specific qualities that you find unattractive. On the right side of the paper, list ten or more of these undesirable qualities. Write down as many qualities as you like, but don't stop before reaching ten.

When you have completed both lists, think again about the person you find attractive and identify at least three unattractive traits in that person. Then think about the person you found unattractive and identify three traits that are relatively appealing.

Now you should have at least twenty-six qualities listed on the page. Read over each one and circle every quality that you own yourself. For example, if you wrote *compassionate* about the attractive person, ask yourself if you are ever compassionate. If so, then circle that word. Don't think too much about it— just respond to your first impressions. Go through all words on both lists and circle every word that describes a quality that you can identify in your own nature.

Look at the list again. For every word that you did not circle, identify the ones that are absolutely inapplicable to you, words that definitely do not describe you. Put a checkmark next to those.

Finally, go back and look at the words that you

circled and identify the top three that describe you most strongly. Turn the paper over and write down those three words. Then go back and look at the words that you *checked* and identify the top three that define you the very least—ones that in no way whatsoever apply to you. Write those three words on the back of the paper under the three words that apply to you the most. Read those six words—the three that describe you best and the three that least apply—out loud. *You are all of these qualities and traits.* The qualities you most strongly deny in yourself are also part of you and are likely the qualities that create the most turbulence in your life. You will attract people with all six of these qualities—the extremely positive qualities because you may not feel that you deserve them and the extremely negative ones because you refuse to acknowledge their presence in your life.

Once you can see yourself in others, it will become much easier to connect with them, and through that connection to discover unity consciousness. The door to synchrodestiny will open. Such is the power of the mirror of relationship.

Exercise 4

NAMASTE

The Sanskrit word *namaste* (pronounced nah-mah-STAY) means "The spirit in me honors the spirit in you." Whenever you first make eye contact with another person, say "Namaste" silently to yourself. This is a way of acknowledging that the being there is the same as the being here.

When you do this, everything about you—your body language, your expression, and your tone—will be recognized by the other person at some profound level. Even though this greeting is silent, the other person will consciously or unconsciously register the respect implicit in your greeting. Practice this exercise for a few days, and see if you notice a difference in your interactions with other people.

THE THIRD PRINCIPLE: MASTER YOUR INNER DIALOGUE

SUTRA: Sat Chit Ananda (*saht chit ah-NAN-dah*)
My inner dialogue reflects the fire of my soul.

THE THIRD PRINCIPLE DESCRIBES HOW YOUR MIND creates your reality—and how, by mastering your inner dialogue, you can literally transform reality to create abundance.

The mantra—*sat chit ananda*—tells us that our soul is that place which is spontaneously love, knowingness, and bliss. *Sat* means truth, freedom from all limitations. *Chit* means total knowledge, spontaneous knowing or pure consciousness. *Ananda* means bliss, total happiness, complete fulfillment. So what that phrase really says is, "My soul is free from limitations.

My soul has spontaneous knowing. My soul exists in complete fulfillment."

Inner dialogue is one of our most basic characteristics. This inner dialogue has an important function: By making judgments, it contributes to survival. This person may be dangerous. That fruit may be good to eat. This may not be a good time to ask my boss for a raise. Useful though it is, this little voice would have you believe that you and it are one and the same, that its goals are your goals. But as we've seen, there is another place inside you where the silent witness dwells. This is the place where you connect to spirit, where the local mind gives way to the nonlocal mind. This is the place you can access through meditation.

INNER DIALOGUE AND
SELF POWER

Being synchronized with the intelligence field creates balance physically, emotionally, and spiritually. It gives you strength and flexibility that allow you to meet any challenge effortlessly. You become capable of transforming the challenge in such a way that it nourishes you, and you draw greater strength from meeting the challenge.

When we find ourselves looking at the world and saying, "There's nothing out there for me," we should probably also look into our hearts and ask, "If there's nothing out there, is there anything in here?" We need to examine our inner dialogue to discover where we might be blocking the conscious energy flow, then remove the ego, step out of the way, and let the fire of the soul shine through us.

If you have fire of soul, then Vedic sages say it is reflected in the shining of your eyes. It's reflected spontaneously in your body language and body movements. Everything you think, feel, say, and do will reflect that same fire. How does it look? There are no absolutes, but the spirit is reflected in impeccable speech and behavior, refraining from anything that could potentially be considered hurtful. The spirit is reflected in confidence, happiness, good humor, fearlessness, kindness, and thoughtfulness. The quality of your inner dialogue is instantly obvious to other people, although it might not be recognized for what it is. When you practice positive inner dialogue, people will want to bond with you, help you, be near you. They want to share in the love, knowingness, and bliss that shines through your eyes and is reflected in your every action. This is true inner power.

Exercise 5

THE FIRE IN YOUR EYES

The fire in your soul will be reflected in your eyes. Whenever you look into a mirror, even if it's just for a second or two, make eye contact with your image and silently repeat the three principles that are the foundation of self-referral. First, say to yourself, "I'm totally independent of the good or bad opinions of others." Second: "I'm beneath no one." Third: "I'm fearless in the face of any and all challenges." Look into your eyes in the mirror and see those attitudes reflected back at you. Just in your eyes, not in your facial expression. Look for the shine in your eyes to remind yourself of the fire in your soul.

THE FOURTH PRINCIPLE:
INTENT WEAVES THE TAPESTRY
OF THE UNIVERSE

SUTRA: San Kalpa (*sahn KAL-pah*)
My intentions have infinite organizing power.

OUR INTENTIONS ARE A MANIFESTATION OF THE
total universe because we are part of the universe. And
our intentions hold within them the mechanics of
their fulfillment. All we really need is clarity of intent. Then if we can get the ego out of the way, the intentions fulfill themselves. Our intentions attract the
elements and forces, the events, the situations, the circumstances, and the relationships necessary to fulfill
the intended outcome. We don't need to become involved in the details—in fact, trying too hard may
backfire. Let the nonlocal intelligence synchronize the

actions of the universe to fulfill your intentions for you. Intention is a force in nature, like gravity, but more powerful. No one has to concentrate on gravity to make it work. No one can say, "I don't believe in gravity," because it is a force at work in the world whether we understand it or not. Intention works the same way.

The only preparation or participation required to unleash the power of intention is a connection to the conscious intelligence field, which can be attained many ways, one of the best being meditation. When a person achieves a certain level of consciousness, whatever he or she intends begins to happen. There are people who are so connected with the conscious intelligence field that their every intent manifests itself—the whole order of the universe orchestrates around it. Of course, it is not strictly true that their every personal intention is being met; in actuality, people who are connected with the conscious intelligence field adopt the intentions of the universe. Their intentions are being met, but that's only because the cosmic mind is using their intentions to fulfill its own desires.

Intention is not simply a whim. It requires attention, and it also requires detachment. Once you have created the intention mindfully, you must be able to detach from the outcome, and let the universe handle the details of fulfillment. If you don't, ego gets involved and clouds the process. You'll feel frustrated if your intention isn't realized soon enough.

Of course, the best way to have all your intentions realized is to align your intentions with the cosmic intent, to create harmony between what you intend and what the universe intends for you. Once that congruence comes into being, you'll find that synchronicity takes on a larger role in your life. The best way to create that harmony is by nurturing an attitude of simple gratitude. Acknowledge your gratitude for everything in your life. Part of creating harmony involves abandoning grievances of all kinds. Grievance comes from the ego. Animals don't have any problems with grudges or grievances. It's only among us human beings that intention is so often encumbered by all sorts of emotional baggage. You must let all that go in order to create a pure intention.

Exercise 6

FOCUSING INTENTION

The best way to focus on intentions is to write them down.

Go to a quiet place where you are not likely to be

disturbed. Write down what you want on all different levels of desire. Include material, ego gratification, relationship, self-esteem, and spiritual desires. Be as specific as possible.

Add or subtract from the list as your desires change or become fulfilled.

Meditate on what life would be like if all these desires were to manifest. See if you can create inner visions of genuine fulfillment on both material and spiritual levels. Don't be concerned about having these visions in any kind of order, or whether they're very realistic or not. Just see them all happening—feel them with all your five senses. The goal is to have congruent attention on all these four levels of aspiration. When that kind of congruency is in play, the internal dialogue is very powerful and clear, and will help you gain unity of consciousness.

Intentions do not need constant attention, but they do need to remain focused. This is a habit that you develop over time. Look at your list once or twice during the day. Read it over again just before you meditate. When you go into meditation, you silence the self. The ego disappears. As a result, you detach from the results and outcomes, you don't get involved in the details, and you let the infinite organizing power of the deeper intelligence orchestrate and fulfill all the details of your intentions for you. The key is to move away from the level of the ego, away from the level of the self and self-esteem, to let the nonlocal intelligence orchestrate the fulfillment of your desires through synchronicity.

In the beginning, you can be as selfish as you want. In the beginning your intentions may be all about "self" and the little details of what you want to happen in your life. But eventually you will realize that the goal is fulfillment at all levels, not just the personal or ego level. As you start to see the fulfillment of your intentions, your self-interest will diminish because you know you can have it all. When you have enough food to eat, you don't obsess about eating all the time. It's the same with intentions. When you know that fulfillment is possible, you will think less about your personal needs and more about the needs of the rest of the world. This is a process that works through stages. Be patient, but watch for the miracles to begin.

THE FIFTH PRINCIPLE: HARNESS YOUR EMOTIONAL TURBULENCE

SUTRA: Moksha (*MOKE-shah*)

I am emotionally free.

ONCE WE UNDERSTAND THAT EXTERNAL REALITY can't be separated from internal reality, once we understand that the universe really is our extended body, it becomes very clear that negative energy within ourselves is destructive. Emotional turbulence is a major barrier to the spontaneous fulfillment of desire, but it is possible to transform negative energy into a higher level of awareness.

The word *moksha* means "freedom." As this sutra resonates within you, it expresses "I am emotionally free. My soul is disengaged from melodrama. I am free from resentment, grievances, hostility, and guilt. I am free of self-importance. I am free of self-concern. I'm free of self-pity. I can laugh at myself. I see the humor in life." These are all contained in that freedom; if I'm not emotionally free, then I overshadow and cloud the experience of the spirit with the ego, and my best intentions cannot be fulfilled.

Ultimately emotional freedom leads to psychological and spiritual freedom as well. There are really only two emotions: pleasure and pain—either it feels good or it hurts. Most people believe that the two fundamental emotions are love and fear, but these are really just the ways we respond to the potential for pleasure and pain. *Love* means we want to get closer to it because we think it will bring us pleasure. *Fear* means we want to move away because we think it will bring pain.

The optimal and truest condition is one of balance. Any time we have emotional turbulence, we upset our natural internal balance, which can block our spiritual evolution and may even disconnect us from synchronicity. This is not to say that emotions are, in themselves, harmful or to be avoided. As human beings we will always have emotions; these are part of the human condition. But we need to avoid getting stuck on one emotion.

Perhaps the most destructive emotion is anger. Anger motivates us to harm others, moving us in the opposite direction from enlightenment and unity consciousness. Anger clouds any perception of unity. Anger is about only the ego. Rather than moving you forward toward synchronicity and enlightenment, anger pushes you backward, closing you down to the transformative messages of the universe.

The first step to converting emotions is to take responsibility for what you are feeling. In order to take responsibility, you must recognize the emotion. What are you feeling? Where do you feel it in your body? Once you can identify the feeling, witness it. Experience it as objectively as possible, as though you are another person looking in. Anger is triggered by pain. Describe the pain from this objective point of view.

After the pain is identified in these ways, you can begin to express, release, and share the pain. Transform the painful experience into new awareness. Eventually you may even be able to celebrate the pain as another step on your road to spiritual enlightenment. When you embrace the pain in this way, emotional turbulence will disappear and the path to synchronicity again becomes clear.

Exercise 7

DEALING WITH PAIN

This exercise will require about ten minutes of quiet time in a place where you are not likely to be disturbed. Begin by meditating for a few moments.

With your eyes closed, recall some event or situation in the past that was very upsetting to you. Once you've settled on an upsetting situation, try to recall as many details about it as possible. Create a mental movie of exactly what happened.

The first step to dealing with the pain of this situation is to identify exactly what you are feeling. What word best describes how you feel because of this event or situation? Try to come up with a single word that encompasses as many of the feelings as possible, your best description. Now, focus on that word for a few seconds.

Let your attention gradually shift from that word to your body. What physical sensations are you feeling as a result of reliving that emotion? Every emotion has both mental and physical aspects that cannot be separated. Our feelings occur both in our minds and in our bodies at the same instant. Feel the sensations that this incident you are thinking about has created. Notice the physical experience of the emotion, and localize it to a specific spot on your body.

The next step is to express the feeling. Place your hand on the part of your body where you sense that the feeling is located. Out loud, say, "It hurts here." If there is more than one location for the pain, touch each place and repeat the phrase, "It hurts here."

For every emotional hurt, we have the power within us to make the pain disappear. Our reactions to external events localize in our bodies. We create emotions, which create physical pain. When we understand that simple fact, we can learn to change the way we respond to outside events. We can choose the way we react to incidents in the world. If we react with anger, hostility, depression, anxiety, or another intense emotion, our bodies follow along and create the necessary hormones and muscle contractions and other physical manifestations that eventually cause us actual pain. Therefore, we must always remember that these effects are our responsibility in the sense that we can change our reactions in ways that are less personally harmful. We can become free of emotional drama and turbulence. Meditate for a moment on the concept of personal responsibility for emotional reactions.

Once the pain has been located and acknowledged, and after you've taken responsibility for it, you can release the pain. Place your attention on the part of your body where you are holding the pain. With every exhalation of breath, have the intention of releasing that tension that you are holding. For half a minute, focus on releasing tension and pain with every breath. Let it go. Breathe it out.

The next step is to share the pain. Imagine that you could speak to the person who was involved in the incident that you have recalled for this exercise. What would you say to that person? As you consider this, remember that the person was not the true cause of your pain. You had the emotional reaction that manifested in physical pain. You have taken responsibility. Knowing this, what would you say to that person? What you choose to say will be personal to you and your situation. Whatever you say to share the pain you experienced will help to cleanse the experience from your consciousness forever. Share what you felt, share how you feel now, and share how you intend to deal with such feelings in the future.

This exercise can be used whenever you feel emotional turbulence in your life. When you have completed the exercise, take a moment to celebrate that you have used this painful experience to transcend to a higher level of consciousness. If you use this exercise consistently, you will eventually be able to entirely free yourself of emotional turbulence and pain, freeing your way to experience synchronicity.

Exercise 8

HEALING CHILDHOOD ANGER

For this exercise, you will need approximately ten minutes of uninterrupted time.

Think back to yesterday. Imagine that your memory is a videocassette that you can rewind to any time you choose. Right now, take it back just twenty-four hours. What were some of the things you did during the day? Did anything frighten you or make you angry? It doesn't have to be anything especially important or dramatic—you may have felt impatient waiting in line, or you might have witnessed someone being rude or inconsiderate. For the next minute or so, try to remember the events of the day in as much detail as you can. Focus on a moment of anger, becoming aware of the sensations in your body as well as the emotions in your mind.

Next, rewind that videotape back even farther. Think back exactly one year. Try to recall what you were doing a year ago on this date, or as close to it as you can remember. What was on your mind at that time? Do you recall being worried or angry about something? Try to feel the emotions of that time in your mind and in your body. Are the feelings the same as the feelings you remember feeling yesterday?

Rewind the tape even farther back to when you were a teenager. Again, focus on a situation that made you angry or frightened. Notice how the anger that you experienced yesterday has been built on emotions from so long ago.

Try now to remember an incident from childhood. What is the earliest time in your life that you can recall being really angry? Bring that experience into your awareness. Where were you when it happened? Who else was there? Who or what was it that made you so angry? Feel all the sensations created by that anger.

Notice how the fear and anger have accumulated over the years. Although you cannot remember it, there was a time in your life before you ever felt anger or fear, a time of total peace and tranquillity. Try to imagine what that experience of utter bliss might have been like. Focus on a time before fear or anger. Rewind that imaginary tape of your life until the screen goes black, and feel the boundaries evaporate between yourself and your surroundings. For the next minute, feel the total loss of all your accumulated anger, fear, and ego.

With that feeling of total bliss still in your awareness, begin to move that imaginary videotape forward again. Visit the same points in your life that you stopped at earlier—those angry or fearful moments from your childhood, your teenage years, a year ago, yesterday. As you envision these scenes again, introduce the experience of bliss back into the setting. Instead of allowing one moment of anger to build upon another, begin to erase these moments one by one, from earliest childhood to just yesterday. Spend a minute or so feeling the anger and fear being erased by this memory of bliss. And as those feelings are erased, allow the toxic buildup of years of anger and fear to be erased from your spirit.

You can use this exercise at any time to attack the anger problem at its roots. Many people find it especially useful at night, just before they go to sleep, so they wake up blissful and without residual anger.

THE SIXTH PRINCIPLE: CELEBRATE THE DANCE OF THE COSMOS

SUTRA: Shiva-Shakti (*SHE-vah SHOCK-tee*)
I am giving birth to the gods and goddesses inside me;
they express all their attributes and powers through me.

THE SIXTH PRINCIPLE ENCOURAGES US TO LIVE
life fully by embracing both the masculine and the
feminine aspects of our being.

One way to embrace both aspects of your self is to
call upon both masculine and feminine archetypes.
According to Carl Jung, archetypes are inherited
memories represented in the mind as universal symbols, and can be observed in dreams and myths. They
are states of awareness. Archetypes are universal con-
centrations of psychic energy.

Archetypes exist as potential and lie dormant in

your consciousness. Everyone has at least one archetype, which stays dormant until triggered by some situation in the environment or in the conscious or unconscious mental life of a person. Once triggered, the archetype will manifest its powers and attributes through you. What you do with your life is usually a representation to some extent of the combination of your archetypes. For example, a person who wields exceptional power in the world, such as a king or a president, will likely have Zeus or Hera as archetypes of power and leadership. But if that person is also exceptionally wise, he or she might also have Athena as an archetype of wisdom.

It is possible to consciously trigger your archetype through intent. Once you discover your primary archetypes, you can begin to call them to you daily. Surround yourself with symbols, words, or representations that remind you of your archetypes. With such symbols next to your bed, let these be the first things you look at when you wake up in the morning. Ask your archetypes for their guidance and wisdom, and ask that they become part of you and work through you. This can be as simple as saying, "I ask that you become part of me and work through me. Guide me through my life."

If you invite your archetypes in this way just after

your daily meditation, you will start to feel their presence more strongly and more directly. They can provide access to the hidden strengths within you.

Exercise 9

FINDING THE COSMOS WITHIN

Read this into a tape and play it to yourself.

Sit or lie comfortably with your eyes closed. Quiet your internal dialogue by observing your breath.

After a few minutes put your attention on your heart. Visualize your heart as a pulsating sphere of light. In this sphere visualize two or three divine beings or archetypal energies. These could be angels, gods, or goddesses. Now visualize the rest of your body also as a body of light. Now slowly imagine this light body with its pulsating sphere of divine beings expanding so it fills the entire room in which you are sitting or lying. Allow the expansion to occur beyond the confines of the room so that you are no longer in the room but in fact the room is in you. Continue the process of expanding your light body so that the entire city in which you live exists in your being—the buildings, the people, the traffic, and the countryside.

Continue to expand your sense of self to include

in your physical being the state in which you live, your country, and ultimately the entire planet. Now see that the whole world exists in you.

Now quietly say to yourself, "I am not in the world; the world is in me." Whatever imbalances you see in this world of yours, ask the divine beings still dancing in your pulsating sphere of a heart to correct them. Ask these divine beings to fulfill any desire you have and to bring harmony, beauty, healing, and joy to the different parts of your cosmic self. Continue to expand your sense of self to include planets and moons, stars and galaxies.

Now say to yourself, "I am not in the universe; the universe is in me." Slowly begin to diminish the size of your cosmic self until you can once again experience your personal body. Imagine trillions of cells in your personal body—all part of a dance, each cell an entire universe unto itself. Remind yourself that your true being inhabits all these levels of creation, from microcosm to macrocosm, from the atom to the universe, from your personal body to your cosmic body. Express your gratitude to these archetypal energies.

Now just remain sitting or lying quietly, feeling all the sensations in your body. You may feel tingling or exhilaration. After two or three minutes, open your eyes. The exercise is over.

14

THE SEVENTH PRINCIPLE:
ACCESSING THE CONSPIRACY
OF IMPROBABILITIES

SUTRA: Ritam (*REE-tahm*)

I am alert, awake to coincidences, and know that they
are messages from God. I flow with the cosmic dance.

THE SEVENTH PRINCIPLE INCORPORATES ALL THE
other aspects of synchrodestiny to form an approach
to life that comes from peaceful awareness.

Ritam means "I am alert to the conspiracy of improbabilities."

Every event has a particular likelihood of happening, or probability. The probability of winning the
lottery is very low. The probability of winning the
lottery without buying a ticket is even lower.

We maximize the probability that something will

happen by our actions. And many of our actions are determined by our karmic conditioning—those interpretations of past experiences and relationships that form and affect our life's memories and desires. If we have had past experiences of being lucky, the probability of buying a lottery ticket increases. But a person who has never won anything feels defeated even before the ticket is purchased, and may never buy the ticket at all.

In order to change your life, therefore, you must break free of your present karmic conditioning. You must transform yourself into the person for whom the probability of great things happening increases. And this transformation starts at the level of the soul. The soul gives meaning to events. The soul takes actions by influencing our minds. And for every action, there is a memory, an interpretation. Meaning, experience, interpretation, memory, desire—all of these are very closely connected through the karmic cycle.

WE GET USED to a certain way of doing things and continue that pattern out of habit, simply because it is comfortable. In order to change your life, you have to find a way to break the pattern. This is not easy, but people do it every day. The best way is to watch for signs of new probabilities—and those signs come to us in the form of coincidences.

Coincidences are messages from the nonlocal domain, invitations to break our karmic bonds. Coincidences invite us to relinquish the known and embrace the unknown. A coincidence is a creative, quantum leap in the behavior of the universe itself. Since the known is itself a habit of past conditioning, creativity and freedom exist in the unknown—anything that breaks through the probability amplitude set by karma. That is why it is important to look for coincidences, to keep a record of them. When you notice coincidences, you can discover their hidden meanings for your life.

A coincidence is, by definition, a synchronistic experience. It comes from the nonlocal domain, and affects our world in unpredictable ways. The very fact that it's a coincidence means that it is a message from God. We must take heed, and then take action. This is our opportunity for a creative response. The goal of enlightenment is to go beyond the probability pattern and experience true freedom. This is why it is important to never ignore a coincidence. Never pass up a chance to see what the universe has planned for you. And if you pay attention to coincidences, you'll find that they accelerate, creating even more opportunities.

This is the secret of synchrodestiny. All the ideas presented here are the ruling principles of the universe. If you make them the guideposts of your own life, you live the life of your dreams. Understanding that these principles are not just abstractions, that actually they are operating in everything we do, is really more than just awareness: It's really a kind of celebration. When you have mastered synchrodestiny, when you have learned to synchronize your life with the universe itself, you are celebrating the cosmic dance.

Exercise 10

PUTTING IT ALL TOGETHER

Go to a place where a lot of activity is taking place, such as a shopping mall. Buy something to eat from the food court. Sit on a bench. Close your eyes. With full awareness, taste the food, smell its aroma, and feel its texture. While keeping your eyes closed, pay attention to all the sounds in your environment. What's that music in the background? Christmas carols? The theme song of a movie? Can you tune in to the conversation of the people next to you? Can you hear scattered phrases, words? Do any sounds strike you as attractive, or draw your attention more than others?

Now put your awareness in your body; feel everything around you. The hardness or softness of the bench or sofa—is it wood, or metal, or fabric?

Now open your eyes and observe the scene around you, the people walking, the colors, the shops, the items in the windows, and the art galleries.

Now close your eyes and in your imagination note once again what you have experienced—the tastes, the smells, the textures, the colors and the objects you saw, the sounds you heard. Now pick an item from each of your sensory experiences. An example of these might include the following: strawberry ice cream on your tongue, the smell of baking bread, the touch of craggy rocks under your feet, a beautiful painting of the sun setting over hills, Christmas carols, and the theme song from the James Bond movie *Goldfinger*. Now tell yourself that all these sounds, smells, textures, and tastes are part of a story. Ask yourself what the story is. Ask your nonlocal self to reveal the story to you. Now let go and assume that your nonlocal self will provide the answer in the form of a synchronistic experience.

The exercise above is an actual example of an

experience I had at a shopping mall during Christmastime. One year later I was in Jamaica. I had taken a drive into the countryside. I saw a scene very similar to the picture in the painting—a beautiful sunset over a hill by the ocean. Upon inquiry I learned that this place was called Strawberry Hill and the James Bond movie *Goldfinger* had been shot here. There was a beautiful hotel on Strawberry Hill. I decided to go inside. They had a luxurious spa. The spa director was delighted to meet me, and he told me that he had been looking for me for the last several weeks because he wanted advice on Ayurvedic therapies. We ended up talking about a mutual collaboration. Several years later I also met the owner of the hotel, who was a record company executive. His wife had an illness for which she consulted me, and we became close friends. He helped me with great advice when I produced my first music CD with healing meditations. Many years later our friendships have continued to evolve, and we feel bonded to each other in the spirit of love; we know we are karmically connected.

LIVING SYNCHRODESTINY

I'D LIKE TO RETURN AGAIN TO THE QUESTION I asked at the beginning of the book: If you knew that miracles could happen, what miracles would you wish for?

If you knew you could have it all and do anything you wanted, what would you choose to have and what would you choose to do?

Synchrodestiny allows you to make these miracles happen, without limits, without end. And it does this by gently and progressively nudging you from the local to the nonlocal domain. When we live only in the local domain, we are impoverished. Our spiritual bank accounts are empty. In the local domain, where most of us reside all the time, you can never be sure of what's going to happen next. Here your actions will carry the burden of anxiety. Your thoughts will be clouded with doubt, and your intentions will be blocked by ego concerns.

But using synchrodestiny to get in touch with the nonlocal domain allows you to enter into a realm of infinite creativity and infinite correlation. Here you have inner security; you are free of anxiety, and free to be the person you were meant to be. In the nonlocal domain you have an unlimited supply of knowledge, of inspiration, of creativity, of potential. You have access to an infinite supply of everything the universe has to offer. Whatever else happens in your life, you are calm, secure, and infinitely blessed.

The principles of synchrodestiny offer a direct route to developing your connection with the nonlocal domain. Practice meditation and review the daily Sutra Statements, and in time you will find yourself connected with spirit in a way that makes miracles not only possible, but a natural part of your everyday life.

Like any other worthwhile journey, living synchrodestiny will require some sacrifice on your part. You need to sacrifice your mistaken ideas that the world operates like a well-oiled machine without consciousness. You need to sacrifice your notion that you are alone in the world. You need to sacrifice the myth that a magical life is not possible. Some people live magical lives all the time. They have learned how to get back in touch with the boundless energy that lies at the heart of the universe. They have learned to watch for clues to the intention of the nonlocal expressed through coincidences, and to derive meaning from those clues so they know what actions are needed to increase the probability that wondrous things will happen.

WHAT TO EXPECT FROM SYNCHRODESTINY

Although the ideas presented in this book can be the beginning of a lifetime of personal evolution and fulfillment, it's up to you to choose whether or not to penetrate the conspiracy of improbabilities and find the hidden treasure that lies behind it. You may start on the path to synchrodestiny as a way to attain wealth, or to find more meaningful relationships, or to become successful in your career. Synchrodestiny certainly can do that for you. But the ultimate goal of synchrodestiny is to expand your consciousness and open a doorway to enlightenment. Enjoy the journey. Each stage brings new wonders, new ways of perceiving and living in the world. Think of synchrodestiny as a kind of rebirth or awakening. Just as your waking days are dramatically different and more exciting than being in a deep sleep, so does awakening to the fifth, sixth, or seventh states of consciousness provide an expansion in what you can experience. Through synchrodestiny, you can finally become the person the universe intended you to be—as powerful as desire, as creative as spirit. All it takes is an eagerness to join the cosmic dance, and a willingness to seek the miracles of the soul.

Once these miracles start to increase as part of your experience of life, you will begin to realize that synchrodestiny is just the symptom of a more profound phenomenon. This profound phenomenon is a shift in your identity and an awakening to who you really are. You begin to understand that the real you is not a person at all. The real you is a field of intelligence in which the person you have identified yourself with, all other persons, as well as the environment in which they exist all co-arise and co-evolve as a result of your own self-interactions. You no longer think of the universe as a sum total of separate and distinct particles but as a coherent, unbroken wholeness in which the personality you currently identify with and its thoughts, all other personalities and their thoughts, and all events and relationships are mutually interdependent, interpenetrating patterns—a single behavior of your nonlocal self. You are the luminous mystery in which the entire universe with all its forms and phenomena arises and subsides. When this realization dawns there is a complete transformation of your personal self into your universal self; there is experiential knowledge of immortality, the complete loss of all fear, including the fear of death. You have become a being that radiates love the same way the sun radiates light. You have finally arrived at the place from which your journey began.

ABOUT THE AUTHOR

DEEPAK CHOPRA is the author of more than fifty books translated in over thirty-five languages, including numerous *New York Times* bestsellers in both the fiction and nonfiction categories. Chopra's Wellness Radio airs weekly on Sirius Stars, Channel 102, which focuses on the areas of success, love, sexuality and relationships, well being, and spirituality. He is founder and president of the Alliance for a New Humanity and can be contacted at www.deepakchopra.com. *Time* magazine heralds Deepak Chopra as one of the top 100 heroes and icons of the century, and credits him as "the poet-prophet of alternative medicine." (June 1999).

Enjoy these new bestsellers
by Deepak Chopra

The Book of Secrets
*Unlocking the Hidden Dimensions
of Your Life*
978-1-4000-9834-7
$14.95 paper (Canada: $19.95)

Peace Is the Way
Bringing War and Violence to an End
978-0-307-33981-2
$13.00 paper (Canada: $18.00)

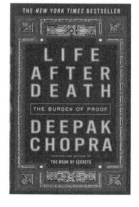

Life After Death
The Burden of Proof
978-0-307-34578-3
$24.00 hardcover (Canada: $32.00)

Available wherever books are sold.